W9-BVY-288

# WHY PRO-LIFE?

# WHY PRO-LIFE?

## RANDY ALCORN

Multnomah® Publishers, Inc.
*Sisters, Oregon*

WHY PROLIFE?
published by Multnomah Publishers, Inc.
© 2004 by Eternal Perspective Ministries

International Standard Book Number: 1-59052-369-5

Cover image by Pixelworks Studio
Interior design and typeset by Katherine Lloyd, The DESK

Scripture quotations are from:
*The Holy Bible,* New International Version
©1973, 1984 by International Bible Society,
used by permission of Zondervan Publishing House

*Multnomah* is a trademark of Multnomah Publishers, Inc.,
and is registered in the U.S. Patent and Trademark Office.
The colophon is a trademark of Multnomah Publishers, Inc.

Printed in the United States of America

ALL RIGHTS RESERVED
No part of this publication may be reproduced, stored in
a retrieval system, or transmitted, in any form or by any
means—electronic, mechanical, photocopying, recording,
or otherwise—without prior written permission.

For information:
MULTNOMAH PUBLISHERS, INC.
POST OFFICE BOX 1720 • SISTERS, OREGON 97759

Library of Congress Cataloging-in-Publication Data

Alcorn, Randy C.
    Why prolife? / Randy Alcorn.
        p. cm.
    Includes bibliographical references.
    ISBN 1-59052-369-5
    1. Abortion--Moral and ethical aspects.  2. Abortion--
Religious aspects--Christianity.  3. Right to life.  I. Title: Why
pro-life?.  II. Title.
    HQ766.15.A53  2004
363.46--dc22
                                                    2004015517

04 05 06 07 08 09 10—10 9 8 7 6 5 4 3 2 1 0

# OTHER BOOKS BY RANDY ALCORN

## FICTION

*Deadline*

*Dominion*

*Edge of Eternity*

*Lord Foulgrin's Letters*

*The Ishbane Conspiracy*

*Safely Home*

## NONFICTION

*In Light of Eternity*

*Money, Possessions & Eternity*

*Law of Rewards*

*ProLife Answers to ProChoice Arguments*

*Restoring Sexual Sanity*

*Sexual Temptation*

*The Grace & Truth Paradox*

*The Purity Principle*

*The Treasure Principle*

*Women Under Stress*

*Heaven*

To Audrey Stout,
who cares for the unborn and their mothers,
and who cared for my mother when she was
dying of cancer in 1981.
Your acts of kindness will not be forgotten
by the God who rewards every cup of
cold water given in His name.

# THANKS...

...to my editor and valued friend, Rod Morris, for his fine touch-up work; Cathy Ramey, who did a great job reducing my original manuscript; and Bonnie Hiestand, who typed in some of the final changes I made on hard copy. Thanks to Brian Smith, Brent Rooney, Kristina Coulter, Kimberly Brock, and Brian Thomasson for their assistance on this project; and to Doug Gabbert for his encouragement. Thanks to my wife Nanci, Ron and Kathy Norquist, Janet Albers, Lind Jeffries, and Sharon Misenhimer. I deeply appreciate each of you for your valuable partnership. Many thanks also to Gayle Atteberry, Larry Gadbaugh, and Alice Gray, who gave me helpful input on the first draft.

# CONTENTS

## Section 4: Other Important Issues

## Section 5: Spiritual Perspectives and Opportunities

Section 1

# THE BASICS

## Chapter 1

# WHY TALK ABOUT ABORTION?

A representative of the National Abortion Rights Action League (NARAL) spoke in a high school class on the merits of abortion. A student asked the teacher if I could come to present the pro-life position. When I arrived a week later, the pro-choice instructor informed me that his students had voted 23-1 for the pro-choice position.

I presented the case for the humanity and rights of unborn children. I showed intrauterine photographs demonstrating the development of the unborn at the earliest stages abortions are performed.

After class, the teacher said to me, "If we were to vote again, the outcome would be different. Minds were changed." Then he added something remarkable: "You know, until today I'd never heard the pro-life position."

We pride ourselves on being open-minded and providing a fair and fact-oriented education. Yet here was a fifty-five-year-old social science teacher with a master's degree who'd *never once heard the pro-life position*. He had uncritically accepted the pro-choice position from others, and his students had done the same.

## THE SURPRISING TREND

Not many years ago it appeared the pro-life position might die of old age. Young people seemed so immersed in moral relativism and tolerance-driven postmodern society that it appeared they would eventually become uniformly pro-choice. But the surprising recent development is that more young people than their parents now oppose abortion.

A recent Gallup survey of teenagers found that 72 percent believe abortion is morally wrong. Only 19 percent believe abortion should be legal in all circumstances, compared to 26 percent of adults. About 32 percent of teens, compared to 17 percent of adults, thought abortion should never be permitted.[1]

This was confirmed by a subsequent national poll,[2] and evidenced by larger numbers of teenagers participating in the national March for Life.[3] Contemporary websites reach out to young women, encouraging them to choose life.[4] Many young people are refusing to accept their culture's defense of abortion.

In *Why ProLife?* I'll present factual and compassionate reasons that explain and validate this movement away from the pro-choice to a pro-life perspective.

## THE DEFINING ISSUE OF OUR AGE

Abortion is America's most frequently performed surgery on women. One out of four children conceived is surgically aborted, with an unknown but growing number of chemical abortions.[5] Since 50 percent of pregnancies are unplanned, this means half of unplanned pregnancies are terminated by abortion. There are about 1.37 million reported abortions in the United States every year.[6] In the U.S., 43 percent of women of childbearing age have had or will have abortions.[7] Virtually every family, at some level, has been touched by abortion.

The stakes in this issue are extraordinarily high. If the pro-choice position is correct, the freedom to choose abortion is a basic civil right. If the pro-life position is correct, the 3,753 abortions occurring every day in America are human casualties, more than all lives lost in the September 11, 2001, destruction of the World Trade Center.

Abortion is the ultimate "hot button." The very word raises powerful emotions. Among issues people feel strongly about, abortion ranks number one—above anti-Semitism, alcohol abuse, homelessness, the death penalty, pornography, and flag burning.[8]

A recent Gallup poll indicated 26 percent of Americans say they are very strongly pro-choice, while 29 percent say they are very strongly pro-life. Taken together, that means 55 percent of Americans hold a very strong view on abortion, and they are almost evenly split in their beliefs.[9]

Since the other 45 percent aren't firm in their opinions, and since many who once felt very strongly have changed their beliefs, likely more than half of Americans can still be influenced in their thinking about abortion.

## A CHRISTIAN PERSPECTIVE

Some Christian readers may think, "This book isn't for us—it's unchurched people who are having abortions." In fact, 43 percent of women obtaining abortions identify themselves as Protestant, and 27 percent identify themselves as Catholic. So two-thirds of America's abortions are obtained by those with a Christian affiliation. Eighteen percent of all U.S. abortions are performed on women who identify themselves as born-again or evangelical Christians.[10] That's nearly a quarter-million abortions each year in Bible-believing churches.

The abortion issue isn't about the church needing to speak to the world. It's about the church needing to speak to itself first, and *then* to the world.

Though I'm a Christian, I don't make many arguments from the Bible in this book. (I've done that elsewhere.[11]) The case I present is grounded in medical science and reliable psychological studies. These sources should be as credible to any truth-respecting agnostic as they are to Christians. Indeed, many non-Christians oppose abortion.

I'm a strong believer in women's rights. I have the deepest respect for my wife and my daughters, whom we raised to respect themselves and to be grateful God made them female. I don't want to understate the trauma women have gone through in making abortion-related decisions. No one understands suffering like Jesus Christ, who is full of grace and truth. The chapter on finding God's forgiveness (chapter 18) is one I need as much as anyone.

This book presents facts and logic, infused with grace and compassion, that can help us root our beliefs in reality.

## MY REQUEST OF READERS

If you are pro-choice and reading a book titled *Why ProLife?* then good for you. I hope this means you have an open mind. If the pro-life side proves to be as senseless and irrational as you may have been led to believe, fine. You can give it the firsthand rejection it deserves. But if it proves to be sensible, then I encourage you to rethink your position.

If you're one of those many who are on the fence, with mixed feelings, I ask you to make this book part of a quest for truth. You can hear the pro-choice position anywhere—just turn on a TV or read the newspaper. But this may be your only opportunity to examine the pro-life position.

If you are pro-life, I ask you to think through your position. It isn't good enough to say, "I know I'm right, but I'm not sure why." We should base our beliefs on the evidence. If we're wrong on any point, by all means let's revise our position. If we're right, we need to learn how to intelligently and graciously inform others.

One thing is certain: If abortion really does kill children and harm women, then there's too much at stake to stand on the fringes and do nothing.

## Chapter 2

# PRO-WOMAN
# OR PRO-CHILD?

My wife and I became involved in pro-life work out of concern for women who'd been devastated by abortion. In 1981 we opened our home to a pregnant teenage girl. I served on the board of one of the first pregnancy centers on the West Coast, offering help to pregnant women who were needy, confused, and desperate. Our objective was to help women in every way possible. And the best way to help these women was to provide them alternatives to abortion.

As time went on, I became involved in pro-life education, political action, and peaceful nonviolent intervention outside abortion clinics. Some pro-life ministries focus more on saving unborn children, others more on helping pregnant women. I found both kinds of efforts to be vitally necessary and completely compatible.

## THE MOVEMENT YOU MAY NOT KNOW

Countless myths have been attached to the pro-life movement. One example is the oft-repeated statement,

"Pro-lifers don't really care about pregnant women, or about children once they're born." A television reporter, with cameras rolling, approached me at a pro-life event and asked for my response to that accusation. I said, "Well, my wife and I opened our home to a pregnant girl and paid her expenses while she lived with us. We supported her when she decided to give up the child for adoption. And, since you asked, we give a substantial amount of our income to help poor women and children."

Then I introduced her to a pastor friend standing next to me who, with his wife, had adopted nineteen children, a number of them with Down syndrome and other special needs. The reporter signaled the cameraman to stop filming. I asked if she wanted to interview my friend. She shook her head and moved on.

The fact is this: Thousands of pro-life organizations around the country and throughout the world provide free pregnancy tests, ultrasounds, counseling, support groups, childcare classes, financial management education, babysitting, diapers, children's clothes, and housing. Add to these tens of thousands of churches donating time, money, food, house repairs, and every other kind of help to needy pregnant women, single mothers, and low-income families. Countless pro-lifers adopt children, open their homes, and volunteer to help children after they're born. Together these efforts comprise the single largest grassroots volunteer movement in history.

While those who offer abortions charge women for them, those who offer abortion alternatives give their assistance freely, lovingly, and almost entirely behind the scenes. Contrary to some caricatures, these people are not just pro-birth—they are pro-*life*. They care about a child and her mother, and are there to help them both not only before birth, but after.

## OUR NATIONAL SCHIZOPHRENIA

Despite an even split among those calling themselves pro-choice and pro-life, two-thirds of Americans say they believe abortion is "morally wrong."[1] Some pro-life advocates have interpreted this to mean it's no longer necessary to argue that the unborn is human or that abortion is wrong. Instead, our emphasis should be on helping women to see that abortion isn't in their best interests.

I emphatically agree we should help women with unwanted pregnancies see that abortion will hurt them, not help them. Many women believe that abortion is wrong, but that it's the least of evils—bad as it is, they think it's still a better alternative to having a baby, raising a child, or surrendering a child for adoption.[2]

We must show them that, while the other alternatives are challenging, abortion is the only one that kills an innocent person. Precisely because it does so, it has by far the most negative consequences in a woman's life.

However, many of the same people who believe unborns are human and that abortion is immoral nonetheless choose to have abortions and defend abortion as legitimate. This proves they do not believe unborns are human beings in the same sense they believe three-year-olds are human beings. They don't believe abortion is immoral in the same way that killing a three-year-old is immoral.

Polls also indicate that many of the same people who believe abortion is immoral nonetheless believe it should remain legal. It's fair to assume that these people believe rape, kidnapping, child abuse, and murder are immoral—but they would *not* argue that rape and murder should be legal. This demonstrates a fundamental difference between what they mean by rape and murder being "immoral" and abortion being "immoral."

No one who considers a preborn child a full-fledged person can rationally defend abortion's legality, unless they also defend legalizing the killing of other human beings. After all, every argument for abortion that appeals to a mother's inconvenience, stress, and financial hardship can be made just as persuasively about her twelve-year-old, her husband, or her parents. In many cases older children are *more* expensive and place greater demands on their mother than an unborn child. But people immediately recognize those arguments are invalid when it comes to killing older children.

Women often say that when they got abortions they had no idea who was inside them. Some knew subconsciously they were carrying a child, but they latched onto dehumanizing pro-choice rhetoric. They now profoundly regret this. They think of what they did as temporary insanity, enabled by their well-intentioned but misguided friends or family. They wish someone would have tried to talk them out of a choice that now haunts them.

We should love and care for pregnant women who feel pressured toward abortion. We should also love women who've had abortions, and do all we can to help them recover from abortion's trauma.

The ancient book of Proverbs says that the right choice is always wise and brings good consequences, while the wrong choice is always foolish and brings bad consequences.

## THE FALSE DICHOTOMY

It's never in anyone's best interests to kill a child. When a child is hurt by his mother it brings harm not only to the child but to her. It's impossible to separate a woman's welfare from her child's. Precisely because the unborn is a child, the consequences of killing him are severe. It's the identity of the first victim, the child, that brings harm to the second victim, the mother. That's why we need to begin our treatment of abortion with the identity of the unborn.

Section 2

# THE
# CHILD

## Chapter 3

# IS THE UNBORN REALLY A HUMAN BEING?

Pro-choice advocates once commonly stated, "It's uncertain when human life begins; that's a religious question that cannot be answered by science." Most have abandoned this position because it's contradicted by decades of scientific evidence. However, this out-of-date belief is so deeply engrained in our national psyche that it's still widely believed.

The only way pro-choice logic can prevail is if people believe the unborn are less than fully human.

Are they?

## WHAT SCIENCE SAYS

Dr. Alfred M. Bongioanni, professor of obstetrics at the University of Pennsylvania, stated, "I have learned from my earliest medical education that human life begins at the time of conception…human life is present throughout this entire sequence from conception to adulthood…any interruption at any point throughout this time constitutes a termination of human life."

Speaking of the early stages of a child's development in the womb, Professor Bongioanni said, "I am no more prepared to say that these early stages represent an incomplete human being than I would be to say that the child prior to the dramatic effects of puberty is not a human being. This is human life at every stage."[1]

Dr. Jerome LeJeune, then genetics professor at the University of Descartes in Paris, stated, "After fertilization has taken place a new human being has come into being." He said, this "is no longer a matter of taste or opinion. Each individual has a very neat beginning, at conception."[2]

Professor Micheline Matthews-Roth of Harvard University Medical School said, "It is scientifically correct to say that an individual human life begins at conception."[3]

The moment of each person's creation is the moment of his conception. Before that moment the individual (with his unique DNA) did not exist. From that moment he does exist.

It's not merely pro-life people who believe this. The owner of Oregon's largest abortion clinic testified under oath, "*Of course* human life begins at conception."[4] The award-winning secular book *From Conception to Birth* documents the child's beginning at conception and his movement toward birth.[5]

How clear is the proof that human life begins at conception? So clear that the Missouri General Assembly overwhelmingly approved a 2003 bill which stated, "The general assembly of this state finds that: (1) The life of each human being begins at conception; (2) Unborn children have protectable interests in life, health, and well-being.... The term 'unborn children' or 'unborn child' shall include all unborn child or children or the offspring of human beings from the moment of conception until birth at every stage of biological development."[6]

## COMPLEX AND HUMAN

The newly fertilized egg contains a staggering amount of genetic information, sufficient to control the individual's growth and development for his entire lifetime. A single thread of DNA from a human cell contains information equivalent to a library of one thousand volumes.[7]

The cells of the new individual divide and multiply rapidly, resulting in phenomenal growth. There's growth because there's life. Long before a woman knows she's pregnant there is within her a living, growing human being.

Between five and nine days after conception the new person burrows into the womb's wall for safety and nourishment. Already his or her gender can be determined by scientific means. By fourteen days the child produces a hormone that suppresses the mother's menstrual period. It will be two more weeks before clearly human features are discernible, and three more before they're obvious. Still, he is a full-fledged member of the human race.

At conception the unborn doesn't appear human to us who are used to judging humanity by appearance. Nevertheless, in the objective scientific sense he is every bit as human as any older child or adult. He looks like a human being ought to at his stage of development.

At eighteen days after conception the heart is forming and the eyes start to develop. By twenty-one days the heart is pumping blood throughout the body. By twenty-eight days the unborn has budding arms and legs. By thirty days she has a brain and has multiplied in size ten thousand times.

By thirty-five days, her mouth, ears, and nose are taking shape. At forty days the preborn child's brain waves can be recorded and her heartbeat, which began three weeks earlier, can already be detected by an ultrasonic stethoscope. By forty-two days her skeleton is formed and her brain is controlling the movement of muscles and organs.

No matter how he or she looks, a child is a child. And, always, abortion terminates that child's life. The earliest means to cause abortion, including Mifepristone (RU-486) and all abortion pills, are too late to avoid taking a life.

## The Drama of Life

Famous intrauterine photographer Lennart Nilsson is best known for his photo essays in *Life* magazine and his book *A Child Is Born.* In his "Drama of Life Before Birth," he says this of the unborn at forty-five days after conception (before many women know they're pregnant): "Though the embryo now weighs only 1/30 of an ounce, it has all the internal organs of the adult in various stages of development. It already has a little mouth with lips, an

early tongue and buds for 20 milk teeth. Its sex and reproductive organs have begun to sprout."[8]

By eight weeks hands and feet are almost perfectly
formed. By nine weeks a child will bend fingers around an
object placed in the palm. Fingernails are forming and the
child is sucking his thumb. The nine-week baby has
"already perfected a somersault, backflip and scissor kick."[9]

The unborn responds to stimulus and may already be
capable of feeling pain.[10] Yet abortions on children at this
stage are called "early abortions."

By ten weeks the child squints, swallows, and frowns.
By eleven weeks he urinates, makes a wide variety of facial
expressions, and even smiles.[11] By twelve weeks the child
is kicking, turning his feet, curling and fanning his toes,
making a fist, moving thumbs, bending wrists, and opening his mouth.[12]

All this happens in the first trimester, the first three
months of life. In the remaining six months in the womb
nothing new develops or begins functioning. The fully
intact child only grows and matures—unless her life is lost
by miscarriage or taken through abortion.

It's an indisputable scientific fact that each and every
surgical abortion in America stops a beating heart and
stops already measurable brain waves.

What do we call it when a person no longer has a
heartbeat or brain waves? Death.

What should we call it when there *is* a heartbeat and there
*are* brain waves? Life. Every abortion ends a human life.

## SLED

Scott Klusendorf says, "The answer to the question, 'What is it?' trumps all other considerations."[13] He points out that there are only four differences between a pre-born and a newborn. They can be remembered through the acronym SLED,[14] which I'll briefly summarize:

*Size:* Does how big you are determine who you are?

*Level of development:* Are twenty-year-olds more human than ten-year-olds, since they are smarter and stronger?

*Environment:* Does being inside a house make you more or less of a person than being outside? Does being located in his mother's body rather than outside make a child less human?

*Degree of dependency:* Does dependence upon another determine who you are? Is someone with Alzheimer's or on kidney dialysis less of a person? Am I, an insulin-dependent diabetic, less of a person than before I contracted the disease?

A three-month-old is much smaller than a ten-year-old, far less developed, and just as incapable of taking care of himself as an unborn.

The question is not how old or big or smart or inconvenient the unborn are, but *who* they are.

The answer is simple—they are human beings.

## Chapter 4

# WHAT'S THE DIFFERENCE BETWEEN EGG, SPERM, EMBRYO, AND FETUS?

T wo years before abortion was legalized in America, a pro-choice advocate instructed nurses in a prominent medical journal, "Through public conditioning, use of language, concepts and laws, the idea of abortion can be separated from the idea of killing."[1] The same year a Los Angeles symposium offered this training: "If you say, 'Suck out the baby,' you may easily generate or increase trauma; say instead, 'Empty the uterus,' or 'We will scrape the lining of the uterus,' but never, 'We will scrape away the baby.'"[2]

Language isn't just the expression of minds but the molder of minds. How words are used influences our receptivity to an idea—even an idea that, communicated in straightforward terms, would be abhorrent.

Words that focus on the pregnancy and the uterus draw attention away from the person residing in the uterus. But no matter how we say it, "evacuating the uterus" or "terminating a pregnancy" is taking a human life.

One pro-life feminist says, "Pro-lifers don't object to

terminating pregnancies. Pregnancies are only supposed to last a short while. We favor terminating them at around nine months. The objection is to killing children."[3]

## WHAT DOES *FETUS* MEAN?

Like *toddler* and *adolescent,* the terms *embryo* and *fetus* don't refer to nonhumans but to humans at particular stages of development. *Fetus* is a Latin word variously translated "offspring," "young one," or "little child."

It's scientifically inaccurate to say a human embryo or a fetus is not a human being simply because he's at an earlier stage of development than an infant. This is like saying that a toddler isn't a human being because he's not yet an adolescent. One of my daughters is two years older than the other. Does this mean she's two years better? Does someone become more human as they get bigger? If so, then adults are more human than children, and football players are more human than jockeys. Something nonhuman doesn't become human by getting older and bigger; whatever is human is human from the beginning.

## IS EGG OR SPERM A PERSON?

Carl Sagan ridiculed abortion opponents by asking, "Why isn't it murder to destroy a sperm or an egg?"[4] The answer, as every scientist should know, is that there is a fundamental difference between sperm and unfertilized eggs on the one hand, and fertilized eggs or zygotes on the other.

Like cells of one's hair or heart, neither egg nor sperm

has the capacity to become other than what it is. But when egg and sperm are joined, a new, dynamic, and genetically unique human life begins. This life is neither sperm nor egg, nor a simple combination of both. A fertilized egg is a newly conceived human being. It's a person, with a life of its own, on a rapid pace of self-directed development. From the instant of fertilization, that first single cell contains the entire genetic blueprint in all its complexity. This accounts for every detail of human development, including the child's sex, hair and eye color, height, and skin tone.[5] Take that single cell of the just conceived zygote, put it next to a chimpanzee cell, and "a geneticist could easily identify the human. Its humanity is already that strikingly apparent."[6]

Product of conception, or POC, is a common depersonalization of the unborn child. In reality, the infant, the ten-year-old, and the adult are all "products of conception," no more nor less than the fetus. As the product of a horse's conception is always a horse, the product of human conception is always a human.

The debate about embryonic stem cells is an example of semantic power. Stem cells are versatile master cells from which a variety of tissues and organs develop. Considered prime materials for biomedical research, they're available from benign human sources, including consenting adults, umbilical cord blood, and placentas. But many scientists are determined to use stem cells from embryonic human babies, who lose their lives in the harvesting. This ethical debate has serious implications for how we view human beings and whether they're expendable to serve others.[7]

Interestingly, the National Institute of Health found that the public was reacting against "human embryonic stem cell research," destroying human embryos by experimentation. So the NIH chose a new term to describe exactly the same thing: "human pluripotent stem cell research." The new term masks the reality that human embryos are the objects of experimentation.[8] Rather than discontinue an unethical procedure, they found another name.

## No Doubts

If human cloning ever succeeds, a person would enter the life continuum at a point after conception. This would do nothing to change their human status. It's a person's presence on the human life continuum, not how they arrived there, that matters.

Dr. Thomas Hilgers states, "No individual living body can 'become' a person unless it already is a person. No living being can become anything other than what it already essentially is."[9]

Abortion providers have become more direct in admitting what happens in an abortion. Dr. Warren Hern, who teaches doctors how to perform abortions, describes his work:

I began an abortion on a young woman who was 17 weeks pregnant…. Then I inserted my forceps into the uterus and applied them to the head of the fetus, which was still alive, since fetal injection is not done at that stage of pregnancy. I closed the forceps, crushing the skull of the fetus, and withdrew the forceps. The fetus, now dead, slid out more or less intact.[10]

This man, who has dedicated his life to performing abortions and teaching others how to do them, has absolutely no doubt that abortion kills a baby.

Do you know something he doesn't?

Chapter 5

# IS THE UNBORN PART
# OF THE WOMAN'S BODY?

s have many others, philosopher Mortimer Adler
claimed that the unborn is "a part of the mother's
body, in the same sense that an individual's arm or
leg is a part of the living organism. An individual's decision to have an arm or a leg amputated falls within the
sphere of privacy—the freedom to do as one pleases in all
matters that do not injure others or the public welfare."[1]

## TRUE OR FALSE?

A body part is defined by the common genetic code it
shares with the rest of its body. Every cell of the mother's
tonsils, appendix, heart, and lungs shares the same genetic
code. The unborn child also has a genetic code, but it is
distinctly different from his mother's. Every cell of his
body is uniquely his, each different from every cell of his
mother's body. Often his blood type is also different, and
half the time his gender is different.

If the woman's body is the only one involved in a pregnancy, then consider the body parts she must have—two

37

noses, four legs, two sets of fingerprints, two brains, two circulatory systems, and two skeletal systems. Half the time she must also have male genitals. If it's impossible for a woman to have male genitals, then the boy she is carrying cannot be part of her body.

A Chinese zygote implanted in a Swedish woman will always be Chinese, not Swedish, because his identity is based on his genetic code, not that of the body in which he resides.

A child may die and the mother live, or the mother may die and the child live, proving they are two separate individuals.[2]

In prenatal surgeries, the unborn, still connected to her mother by the umbilical cord, is removed, given anesthesia, operated on, and reinserted into her mother. The child is called a patient, is operated on, and has her own medical records, indicating blood type and vital signs.

In 1999, an unborn child named Samuel Armas was operated on for spina bifida. His photograph in *Life* magazine captured the world's attention. As the surgeon was closing, Baby Samuel pushed his hand out of the womb and grabbed the surgeon's finger. Photojournalist Michael Clancy caught this astonishing act on film. (See the very similar award-winning *Life* magazine photo of unborn Sarah Marie Switzer on the back cover of this book.) Clancy reported, "Suddenly, an entire arm thrust out of the opening, then pulled back until just a little hand was showing. The doctor reached over and lifted the hand, which reacted and squeezed the doctor's finger. As if testing for strength, the doctor shook the tiny fist. Samuel held firm. I took the picture! Wow!"[3]

Samuel Armas was sewn back into his mother's womb, and then born nearly four months later. How did seeing Samuel grab the surgeon's finger affect Clancy? "In that instant, Clancy went from being pro-choice to being pro-life. As he put it, 'I was totally in shock for two hours after the surgery.... I know abortion is wrong now—it's absolutely wrong.'"[4]

Does anyone seriously believe that this pain-feeling, finger-grabbing patient was simply an appendage of his mother's body? Can it be credibly argued that once he's placed back inside his mother, it should be legal to kill that same patient anytime during the remaining four months until he's born?

## INCONSISTENCIES EVERYWHERE

At the Medical University of South Carolina, if a pregnant woman's urine test indicates cocaine use, she can be arrested for distributing drugs to a minor. Similarly, in Illinois a pregnant woman who takes an illegal drug can be prosecuted for "delivering a controlled substance to a minor." This is an explicit recognition that the unborn is a person with rights, deserving protection even from his mother.

However, that same woman who's prosecuted and jailed for endangering her child is *free to abort that same child*. In America today, it's illegal to harm your preborn child, but it's perfectly legal to kill him.

Every alcohol-serving establishment in Oregon is required to post this sign:

If alcohol harms unborn babies, what does abortion do to them?

The U.S. Congress voted unanimously to delay capital punishment of a pregnant woman until after her delivery. Every congressman, even if pro-choice, knew that this unborn baby was a separate person, innocent of his mother's crime. No stay of execution was requested for the sake of the mother's tonsils, heart, or kidneys.

Many states have passed fetal homicide laws, declaring it murder for anyone but the mother to deliberately take the life of a preborn child. These laws are explicit affirmations that the child is a human being. In 2004 Congress passed the "Unborn Victims of Violence Act," which states that someone who "intentionally kills or attempts to kill the unborn child...be punished...for intentionally killing or attempting to kill a human being."[5]

Consider the bizarre implications of this double standard. If a woman is scheduled to get an abortion, but on her way to the abortion clinic her baby is killed in-utero, the baby's killer will be prosecuted for murder. But if this murder doesn't occur, an hour later the doctor will be paid to perform a legal procedure killing *exactly the same child* (in a way that is probably more gruesome).

To the child, what's the difference who kills her?

## A Lesson from Louise Brown

Being inside something isn't the same as being part of something. (A car isn't part of a garage because it's parked there.) Louise Brown, the first test-tube baby, was conceived when sperm and egg joined in a Petri dish. Did she become part of her mother's body when she was placed in her uterus? No more than she'd been part of the Petri dish when she lived there.

Human beings shouldn't be discriminated against because of their place of residence. There's nothing about birth that makes a baby essentially different than he was before birth. There's no magic that changes a child's nature when she moves twenty inches, from inside her mother to outside.

## Chapter 6

# WHAT DO THE PICTURES TELL US?

The biggest disadvantage to the preborn child has always been that there's no window to the womb. His fate is in the hands of those who cannot see him. But in recent years this has radically changed.

*Time* in 2002 and *Newsweek* in 2003 devoted cover stories to the breathtaking ultrasound images of preborn children.[1] *Newsweek* asked on its cover, "Should a Fetus Have Rights? How Science Is Changing the Debate."

All arguments vaporize in the face of the unborn child.

## THE POWER OF ULTRASOUND

Rebekah Nancarrow received an $80 ultrasound at Planned Parenthood, but wasn't allowed to see the results because "that will only make it harder on you." Unsettled, she went to a Pregnancy Resource Center, where she was given a free ultrasound and allowed to view it. She said, "Had I not had the sonogram, I would have had the abortion. But that sonogram just confirmed 100 percent to me that this was a life within me, not a tissue or a glob."[2]

According to Thomas Glessner, "Prior to ultrasound technology, pregnancy centers reported that of the 'abortion-minded' women who came in for testing and advice, about 20 percent to 30 percent decided to remain pregnant. With pregnancy centers using ultrasound machines, that proportion has jumped to 80 percent or 90 percent."[3]

Audrey Stout, a nurse, told me of an ultrasound she performed. This particular time the baby "opened and closed her mouth, had the hiccups, laid back as if in a beach chair, stretching her little legs. She even held up hands so Mom could count her fingers. The mother was visibly touched."

When Audrey finished the scan she asked the woman what her plans were. "She replied, 'I am going to have my baby.' I asked if the scan had made a difference; she said, 'Big-time. I just came in here to get a pregnancy verification so I could go have an abortion.'"[4]

Thousands of stories like this have emerged from pregnancy centers that now use ultrasounds. Internet sites display astounding ultrasound images—some clearly show the unborn smiling, yawning, stretching, and sleeping.[5]

Still, denial remains surprisingly strong. When I showed an intrauterine photograph of an eight-week unborn child to a pro-choice advocate—an intelligent college graduate—she asked me, "Do you really think you're going to fool anyone with this trick photography?"

I told her she could go to Harvard University Medical

School textbooks, *Life* magazine,[6] or Nilsson's *A Child Is Born*[7] and find exactly the same pictures. She didn't want to hear it. Why? Because she was really saying, "That's obviously a child in this photograph, and because I don't want to believe abortion kills a child, I refuse to believe that's a real photograph."

## WHAT THE REMAINS INDICATE

A film called "The Gift of Choice" claims that the unborn is "a probability of a future person." But what's left after an abortion are small but perfectly formed body parts—arms and legs, hands and feet, torso and head. The physical remains indicate the end not of a potential life but of an actual life. If you don't believe this, examine the remains of an abortion.[8] If you cannot bear to look, ask yourself why. If this were only tissue, rather than a dismembered child, it wouldn't be hard to look at, would it?

In his how-to manual, *Abortion Practice,* Dr. Warren Hern states, "A long curved Mayo scissors may be necessary to decapitate and dismember the fetus."[9] One must have a head in order to be decapitated and body parts in order to be dismembered. Lumps of flesh and blobs of tissue aren't decapitated or dismembered.

Why are the same people who watch bloody killings and gruesome autopsies in prime-time dramas disturbed by abortion photographs? Pro-choice feminist Naomi Wolf, speaking of pictures of aborted babies, acknowledges,

To many pro-choice advocates, the imagery is revolting propaganda. There is a sense among us, let us be frank, that the gruesomeness of the imagery belongs to the pro-lifers…that it represents the violence of imaginations that would, given half a chance, turn our world into a scary, repressive place. "People like us" see such material as the pornography of the pro-life movement. But feminism at its best is based on what is simply true…. While images of violent fetal death work magnificently for pro-lifers as political polemic, the pictures are not polemical in themselves: they are biological facts. We know this."[10]

## THE RIGHT TO REMAIN IGNORANT

When a pro-life candidate ran television ads showing aborted babies, people were outraged. A *CBS Evening News* reporter declared the abortion debate had reached a "new low in tastelessness." Strangely, there was no outrage that babies were being killed…only that someone had the audacity to *show* they were being killed.

The question we should ask is not "Why are pro-life people showing these pictures?" but "Why would anyone defend what's shown in these pictures?" The real concern about pictures of unborn babies isn't that they're gory, but that they prove the accuracy of the pro-life position.

Intrauterine photos and ultrasounds aren't hideous,

but beautiful and fascinating. So do pro-choice advocates welcome *these* pictures? No. Abortion rights organizations have referred to ultrasound images as a "weapon" in the hand of the pro-life movement.[11] Sometimes clinics and businesses now offer Real-Time 3D (sometimes called 4D) ultrasound photographs of unborn children smiling, sneezing, and yawning. (See the ultrasound image of an unborn child on the back cover of this book.) In a PBS discussion, one panelist claimed that such pictures reflected "an unhealthy preoccupation with the baby."[12] Notice the terminology: "the baby." Ultrasound technologies are dismantling the age-old pro-choice argument, "It isn't a baby." People are saying, "What are you talking about? Of course it's a baby—just *look!*"

## OVERCOMING DENIAL

The Holocaust was so evil that words alone couldn't describe it. Descriptions of Nazi death camps had long been published in American newspapers, but when these papers started printing the pictures of slaughtered people, the American public finally woke up. If not for the pictures, even today most of us wouldn't understand or believe the Holocaust.

I visited a college campus where a pro-life group had set up displays of aborted babies alongside the victims of the Nazi death camps, the killing fields, American slavery, and other historical atrocities. Signs with warnings about the graphic photographs were posted clearly, so all those who looked did so by choice. I witnessed the profound effect on students and faculty, including those who didn't want to believe what they were seeing.

Animal rights advocates argue that in order to make their case they must show terrible photographs, such as baby seals being clubbed to death. If there's a place to look at such pictures, isn't there a place to look at pictures of abortions? And if abortion isn't killing babies…then why are these pictures so disturbing?

Was the solution to the Holocaust to ban the disgusting pictures? Or was the solution to end the killing?

Is the solution to abortion getting rid of pictures of dead babies? Or is it getting rid of what's making the babies dead?

## Chapter 7

# WHAT MAKES A HUMAN LIFE "MEANINGFUL"?

D r. William Harrison, a pro-choice advocate, argues, "The real issue in the abortion debate today is not when life begins, but is it morally meaningful life."[1]

But who determines which lives are meaningful and which aren't? The answer, always, is that powerful people decide whether weaker people's lives are meaningful.

## A DOUBLE STANDARD

Peter Singer, the Princeton ethics professor, wrote, "The life of a fetus is of no greater value than the life of a nonhuman animal at a similar level of rationality, self-consciousness, awareness, capacity to feel, etc."[2] (Parents paying for their children to attend Singer's classes might want to consider that he also believes there's moral justification for killing the elderly.)

A Portland, Oregon, abortionist, Jim Newhall, said, "Not everybody is meant to be born. I believe, for a baby, life begins when his mother wants him."[3] So a human life becomes real only when and if another person values it?

In the 1973 *Roe v. Wade* decision the Supreme Court questioned whether the unborn had "meaningful" lives. But *meaningful to whom?* Doesn't every human being regard as meaningful the life he had in the womb, since if it had been terminated, he would not now be alive?

Whites decided that blacks were less human. Men decided women had fewer rights. Nazis decided Jews' lives weren't meaningful. Now big people have decided that little people aren't meaningful enough to have rights.

Personhood isn't something to be bestowed on human beings by Ivy League professors intent on ridding society of "undesirables." Personhood has an inherent value that comes from being a member of the human race. According to the Bible, this is part of being created in God's image.

## WHAT SCIENCE SAYS OF "MEANING"

What constitutes "meaningful" life? It's a scientific fact that there are thought processes at work in unborn babies. The Associated Press reported a study showing "babies start learning about their language-to-be before they are born." Studies show that while in their mothers' wombs, "fetuses heard, perceived, listened and learned something about the acoustic structure of American English."[4]

*Newsweek* states, "Life in the womb represents the next frontier for studies of human development, and the early explorations of the frontier…have yielded startling discoveries."[5] The article says, "With no hype at all, the fetus can rightly be called a marvel of cognition, consciousness and sentience." It also says that scientists have already detected sentience (self-awareness) in the second trimester.[6] The extraordinary capacities of preborn children have been well documented by scientific studies for years.[7]

By early in the second trimester the baby moves his hands to shield his eyes from bright light coming in through his mother's body. "The fetus also responds to sounds in frequencies so high or low that they cannot be heard by the human adult ear."[8] He hears loud music and covers his ears at loud noises from the outside world. At seventeen weeks, the child experiences rapid eye movement (REM) sleep, indicating that he's not only sleeping but dreaming.[9] Can we say that someone capable of dreaming is incapable of thinking?

Undoubtedly, later abortions kill a sentient, thinking human being. By the end of the second trimester the "brain's neural circuits are as advanced as a newborn's."[10] It seems unthinkable that anyone aware of the facts could defend the current legality of abortions in the second and third trimesters. Yet pro-choice advocates adamantly defend such abortions.

But are earlier abortions any better than later ones? Even in the case of early chemical abortions, which take life before there's capacity for thought, death is just as real and significant. A living child who would've had a name, family, and life will now have none of these.

## A FLAWED ETHIC

Singer says, "If we compare a severely defective human infant with a nonhuman animal, a dog or a pig, for example, we will often find the nonhuman to have superior capacities, both actual and potential, for rationality, self-consciousness, communication and anything else that can plausibly be considered morally significant."[11]

Singer suggests that individual human worth is based on its usefulness to others: "When the death of a disabled infant will lead to the birth of another infant with better prospects of a happy life, the total amount of happiness will be greater if the disabled infant is killed. The loss of happy life for the first infant is outweighed by the gain of a happier life for the second. Therefore, if killing the hemophiliac infant has no adverse effect on others, it would, according to the total view, be right to kill him."[12]

When Singer came to teach at Princeton, he was protested by Not Dead Yet, a disabilities rights group. They took offense at Singer's books, which say it should be legal to kill disabled infants, as well as children and adults with severe cognitive disabilities.

Pro-choice logic started with abortion, but it hasn't stopped there. Once it's acceptable to kill unborn children, no one who's weak or vulnerable can be safe. Does the handicapped person have a meaningful life? How about the elderly? If those who cannot think don't deserve to live, what about those who think incorrectly?

Dr. Charles Hartshorne of the University of Texas

echoes Singer's ethic: "Of course, an infant is not fully human.... I have little sympathy with the idea that infanticide is just another form of murder. Persons who are already functionally persons in the full sense have more important rights even than infants."[13]

## IS ANYONE SAFE?

David Boonin argues that abortion is "morally criticizable" yet "morally permissible." It's permissible, he says, because abortion may potentially produce "overall happiness."[14] Like Singer, Boonin overlooks the fact that the same subjective sense of happiness (as measured by convenience and relief of stress or financial hardship) can be achieved by taking the lives of other people, not just the unborn. Once something is regarded as morally permissible because it may appear to produce happiness, there's nothing that can't qualify.

Hidden beneath much of the discussion of what constitutes meaningful life is utilitarianism. Are mentally and physically disabled or disadvantaged people useful to the healthy and powerful, or are they a burden to us? As one feminist group points out, if unborn children are not safe, no one is safe:

> If we take any living member of the species *Homo sapiens* and put them outside the realm of legal protection, we undercut the case against discrimination for everyone else. The basis for equal

treatment under the law is that being a member of the species is sufficient to be a member of the human community, without consideration for race, gender, disability, age, stage of development, state of dependency, place of residence or amount of property ownership.[15]

Abortion has set us on a dangerous course. We may come to our senses and back away from the slippery slope. Or we may follow it to its inescapable conclusion—a society in which the powerful, for their own self-interest, determine which human beings will live and which will die.

University of Chicago biologist Dr. Leon Kass says concerning the direction of modern science and medicine, "We are already witnessing the erosion of our idea of man as something splendid or divine, as a creature with freedom and dignity. And clearly, if we come to see ourselves as meat, then meat we shall become."[16]

This is the world being shaped by the rhetoric of the abortion rights movement.

Is it the world you want your children and your grandchildren to live in?

Section 3

∽

# THE
# WOMAN

## Chapter 8

# IS ABORTION REALLY
# A WOMEN'S RIGHTS ISSUE?

Kate Michelman, former president of NARAL, says: "We have to remind people that abortion is the guarantor of a woman's…right to participate fully in the social and political life of society."[1] But a pregnant woman *can* fully participate in society. And if she can't, isn't the solution changing society rather than killing children?

"How can women achieve equality without control of their reproductive lives?" Feminists for Life responds:

> The premise of the question is the premise of male domination throughout the millennia—that it was nature which made men superior and women inferior. Medical technology is offered as a solution to achieve equality; but the premise is wrong…. It's an insult to women to say women must change their biology in order to fit into society.[2]

In her essay, "Feminism: Bewitched by Abortion," environmentalist Rosemary Bottcher argues that the feminist movement has degraded women by portraying them as unable to handle the stress and pressures of pregnancy without resorting to killing their children.[3]

Pro-choice groups consistently oppose efforts to require that abortion be treated like every other surgery when it comes to informing the patient of its nature and risks. They don't seem to believe that women are capable of making intelligent choices after being presented with the facts.

Serrin Foster, president of Feminists for Life, speaks powerfully in "The Feminist Case Against Abortion." She says that historically the primary activists against abortion were women, and ironically "the anti-abortion laws that early feminists worked so hard to enact to protect women and children were the very ones destroyed by the *Roe v. Wade* decision 100 years later."[4]

## FEMINIST HISTORY

Susan B. Anthony stood for women's rights at a time when women weren't even allowed to vote. She referred to abortion as "child murder" and viewed it as a means of exploiting both women and children. Anthony wrote, "I deplore the horrible crime of child murder.... No matter what the motive, love of ease, or a desire to save from suffering the unborn innocent, the woman is awfully guilty who commits the deed."[5]

Anthony's newspaper, *The Revolution,* made this claim: "When a woman destroys the life of her unborn child, it is a sign that, by education or circumstances, she has been greatly wronged."[6]

Anthony and other feminists who opposed abortion were followed decades later by a new breed of feminists. Most prominent was Margaret Sanger, who advocated abortion as a means of eugenics, economics, and sexual liberation. After eugenics fell into disfavor following the Holocaust, her organization went underground, then later resurfaced as the Planned Parenthood Federation.[7] Sanger and others who followed Anthony tried to tie the abortion agenda to the legitimate issues of women's rights.

Dr. Bernard Nathanson says that in the 1960s, he and his fellow abortion-rights strategists deliberately linked abortion to the women's issue so it could be furthered not on its own merits but on the merits of women's rights.[8] Abortion rode on the coattails of women's rights.

Alice Paul drafted the original version of the Equal Rights Amendment (ERA), a landmark feminist document. But Alice Paul referred to abortion as "the ultimate exploitation of women."[9]

One feminist has labeled the attempt to marry feminism to abortion as "terrorist feminism." In her words, it forces the feminist to be "willing to kill for the cause you believe in."[10] In their publication *The American Feminist,* Feminists for Life features the beautiful face of a child and asks, "Is this the face of the enemy?" They argue that they stand on two hundred years of pro-life feminist history, and that it wasn't until the 1970s that the women's movement embraced abortion.[11]

Polls indicate that more women than men affirm the unborns' right to life.[12] In fact, "the most pro-abortion category in the United States (and also in other nations) is white males between the ages of twenty and forty-five."[13] More specifically, "the group that is most consistently pro-choice is actually single men."[14] It's ironic that abortion has been turned into a women's rights issue when it has encouraged male irresponsibility and failure to care for women and children. Shouldn't men be called upon to do more than just provide money to kill a child? Shouldn't they be encouraged instead to say to the woman they've made pregnant, "I'll be there for our child. I'll do everything I can for her. And if you're willing to have me, I'll be there for you too."

## SEX SELECTION

One of the ironies of feminism is that by its advocacy of abortion it has endorsed the single greatest means of robbing women of their most basic right—the right to life.

Abortion has become the primary means of eliminating unwanted females across the globe. A survey of a dozen villages in India uncovered a frightening statistic: out of a total population of ten thousand, only fifty were girls.[15] The other girls, thousands of them, had been killed by abortion. In Bombay, of eight thousand amniocentesis tests indicating the babies were female, all but one of the girls were killed by abortion.[16]

Because of sex-selection abortions, two-thirds of children born in China are now males. In the countryside, the ratio of boys to girls is four to one.[17]

Amniocentesis is also being used to detect a child's gender in America. *Medical World News* reported a study in which ninety-nine mothers were informed of the sex of their children. Fifty-three of these preborns were boys and forty-six were girls. Only one mother elected to abort her boy, while twenty-nine elected to abort their girls.[18]

More girls than boys are now being killed by abortion. To kill an unborn female is to kill a young woman. There can be no equal rights for all women until there are equal rights for unborn women.

## Chapter 9

# DO WE HAVE THE RIGHT TO CHOOSE WHAT WE DO WITH OUR BODIES?

Pro-choice advocates argue, "Every woman has the right to choose what she does with her own body." Ironically, the choice of abortion assures that at least 650,000 females in the U.S. each year don't have the right to choose what they do with their bodies. (That number is roughly half of aborted children, the other half being males.) A female killed by abortion no longer has a life, a choice, or a body to exercise control over.

A man isn't permitted to expose himself. There are laws against public urination, prostitution, and drug use. Most of us agree with these laws, though they restrict freedom to do certain things with our bodies. My hand is part of my body, but I'm not free to use it to strike you or steal from you or hurt a child.

## THE RIGHT TO CHOOSE

When presenting the pro-life position on school campuses, I've sometimes begun by saying, "I am pro-choice. That's why I believe every man has the right to rape a woman if that's his choice. After all, it's his body, and we don't have the right to tell him what he can and cannot do with it."

After I let the shock settle in, I ask them to tell me the fallacy of my argument. They point out that in asserting the man's right to choose I've ignored the harm done to the innocent woman, whose rights have been violated. I say, "So you're telling me you're anti-choice, is that it?" After they argue more I respond, "So you're saying that if I demonstrate to you that a woman's choice to have an abortion harms or kills another human being, you'll no longer be pro-choice about abortion?"

My hope is that the light will turn on and they will heed their own common sense, which is perfectly sound—but which they've failed to apply to abortion.

It's absurd to defend a specific choice on the basis that it's a choice. The high-sounding "right to choose" ignores the obvious: *not all choices are legitimate*. In fact—and nearly as many non-Christians as Christians will agree—some choices are downright evil. Some choices are good, others are bad. Therefore, we can't be uniformly pro-choice or anti-choice. Rather, we should be pro-good and anti-evil.

## SELECTIVELY PRO-CHOICE

All of us are in favor of free choice when it comes to where people live, what kind of car they drive, what food they eat, and a thousand matters of personal preference. We're also pro-choice in matters of religion, politics, and lifestyle, even when people choose beliefs and behavior we don't like.

But there are many things you are not pro-choice about—including whether someone has the right to choose to assault you, rob you, break into your house, steal your car, or cheat you in a business deal. It's self-evident that people have the *freedom* to make these choices, but that doesn't mean they have the *right* to make them.

When we oppose the "right to choose" rape or child abuse, we aren't opposing a right, we're opposing a wrong. And we're not narrow-minded and bigoted for doing so.

Somehow the "pro-choice" movement, which in fact is the pro-abortion movement, has successfully commandeered the word *choice*. *Choice* is a euphemism for abortion, so arguing against abortion *appears* to be arguing against choice. Pro-lifers must not argue against choice— it's a battle that can't be won and shouldn't be fought. We must not let abortion remain anchored to choice. Rather, whenever we hear "pro-choice" we must ask, and urge others to ask, *What choice are we talking about?* If it's abortion, the question is, *Do you think people should have the right to choose to kill children?* By opposing abortion we are not opposing choice in general, we are opposing *one choice* in particular—child-killing.

Consider the popular pro-choice question, "If you don't trust me with a choice, how can you trust me with a child?" It's intended as a discussion stopper. But notice how *choice* is substituted for *abortion*. When we insert words that reflect reality, the question becomes, "If you don't trust me to kill a child, how can you trust me to raise a child?"

Huh?

## WHAT ABOUT THE VICTIM'S CHOICE?

One woman points out, "After a woman is pregnant, she cannot choose whether or not she wishes to become a mother. She already is…all that is left to her to decide is whether she will deliver her baby dead or alive."[1]

Slave owners were pro-choice. They emphasized physical differences to justify their superiority over the enslaved. They said, "You don't have to own slaves, but don't tell us we can't choose to." Those who wanted slaveholding to be illegal were accused of being anti-choice and anti-freedom, and of imposing their morality on others.[2]

Every movement of oppression and exploitation—from slavery, to prostitution, to drug dealing, to abortion—has labeled itself pro-choice. Likewise, they've labeled opposing movements that offer compassion and deliverance as "anti-choice."

The pro-choice position always overlooks the victim's right to choose. Blacks didn't choose slavery. Jews didn't choose the ovens. Women don't choose rape. And babies don't choose abortion.

# Chapter 10

# IS ABORTION PART OF
# A RIGHT TO PRIVACY?

A bortion is no one else's business. Everyone has a
right to privacy."
Contrary to popular belief, the U. S. Constitution
says nothing of a right to privacy. Furthermore, privacy
is never an absolute right, but is always governed by other
rights.

What would we think of a man who defended wife-
beating or child abuse, saying "What I do privately is no
one's business but mine"?

Another common statement: "Abortion is a private
decision between a woman and her doctor."

Physicians are trained in medicine, but their moral
opinions aren't as authoritative as their medical diagnoses
(which themselves are sometimes flawed). Many doctors
are conscientious people who place human welfare above
expedience and money. Unfortunately, some doctors are
not reliable moral guides.

That physicians are capable of profoundly evil judg-
ments was demonstrated by many German doctors

during World War II. Robert Jay Lifton, in his powerful book *The Nazi Doctors*, documents how intelligent medical professionals participated in cruel and deadly surgeries, and experiments on helpless children, with shocking ease.[1] They were the best-trained medical personnel in Europe, but they lost their moral compass.

Doctors who perform abortions are no more objective about abortion than tobacco companies are objective about cigarette smoking. Their personal and financial vested interests in abortion, as well as the desensitization of their consciences, disqualify them as sources of moral guidance.

## AVOIDING EMBARRASSMENT

Many young women and their parents don't want to be embarrassed in front of critical onlookers.

No matter what one's view of sex outside of marriage, pregnancy per se is not wrong, even if the sexual act that resulted in pregnancy was. No one should treat the mother as a "bad girl" or pressure her to "solve her problem" by aborting her child. We should love her and help her through the pregnancy, offering her guidance as to whether to raise the child or choose adoption. Whichever she chooses, we should support her.

Whenever I see an unmarried woman carrying a child, my first response is appreciation. I know she could have taken the "quick fix" without anyone knowing, but she chose instead to let her child live.

Premarital sex has serious consequences even apart from unwanted pregnancy. For this reason we should enthusiastically endorse abstinence education.[2] Abstinence is saying no to what harms you and in doing so it's saying yes to the life that's best for you. But after it's happened, premarital sex can be learned from, and not repeated. Killing an innocent human being by abortion is more serious and more permanent. It makes one person pay for another's mistake. Furthermore, it forces the young woman to live with guilt, and gives her a worse mistake to cover up. Abortion may temporarily hide a problem, but it never solves it.

Abortion fosters the attitude, "My comfort and happiness come first—even if I have to disregard the rights of an innocent person to get them." This attitude emerges in a thousand arenas, big and small, which cumulatively tear apart the moral fabric of society. (And it never delivers the happiness it promises.)

One person's unfair or embarrassing circumstances do not justify taking the life of another person.

# Chapter 11

# DOES ABORTION HARM A WOMAN'S PHYSICAL AND MENTAL HEALTH?

A bortion has completely failed as a social policy designed to aid women," writes Serrin Foster, president of Feminists for Life. "It is a reflection that we have failed women."[1]

Joan Appleton was an abortion advocate with NOW and head nurse at a Virginia abortion facility. She asked herself why abortion was "such a psychological trauma for a woman, and such a difficult decision for a woman to make, if it was a natural thing to do. If it was so right, why was it so difficult?"

Appleton said to herself, "I counseled these women so well; they were so sure of their decision. Why are they coming back now—months and years later—psychological wrecks?"[2]

Countless women who have been damaged by abortions have said, "I had no idea this could happen; no one warned me about the risks."

## COMMON COMPLICATIONS

In her testimony before a Senate subcommittee in 2004, Dr. Elizabeth Shadigan testified that "abortion increases rates of breast cancer, placenta previa, preterm births, and maternal suicide…. Statistically, all types of deaths are higher with women who have had induced abortions."[3]

At least forty-nine studies have demonstrated a statistically significant increase in premature births or low birth weight risk in women with prior induced abortions. "Low birth weight and premature birth are the most important risk factors for infant mortality or later disabilities as well as for lower cognitive abilities and greater behavioral problems."[4]

The odds of malformations in later children are increased by abortion.[5] The frequency of early death for infants born after their mothers have had abortions is between two and four times the normal rate.[6] Because induced abortion increases the risk of delivering a future baby prematurely, it appears to be responsible for thousands of cases of cerebral palsy in North America.[7]

Ectopic pregnancies occur when gestation takes place outside the uterus, commonly in a fallopian tube. Such pregnancies are responsible for 12 percent of all pregnancy-related maternal deaths.[8] The U.S. Department of Health and Human Services conducted a twenty-year study on ectopic pregnancy rates, which indicated an increase in ectopic pregnancies of more than 500 percent since abortion was legalized.[9]

Studies show that the risk of an ectopic pregnancy is twice as high for women who have had one abortion, and up to four times as high for women with two or more previous abortions.[10] Of those who have an ectopic pregnancy, 40 percent become infertile, and the odds of having another ectopic pregnancy are one in three. Remarkably, "Only 33 percent of women with ectopic pregnancy will have a subsequent live birth."[11]

The Centers for Disease Control (CDC) reports, "Pregnancy-related complications, such as ectopic pregnancy...still affect 2,000 women each day."[12]

Pelvic Inflammatory Disease (PID) is an infection that leads to fever and infertility. Researchers state, "Pelvic infection is a common and serious complication of induced abortion and has been reported in up to 30 percent of all cases."[13] A study of women having first-trimester abortions established that "women with postabortal pelvic inflammatory disease had significantly higher rates of...spontaneous abortion, secondary infertility, dyspareunia, and chronic pelvic pain."[14]

Placenta previa, a misplacement of the placenta, is caused by "prior uterine insult or injury,"[15] including abortion. It's seven to fifteen times more common among women who've had abortions than among those who haven't.[16] "The reported immediate complication rate, alone, of abortion is no less than 10 percent. In addition, studies of long-range complications show rates no less than 17 percent and frequently report complication rates in the range of 25 to 40 percent."[17]

Women with one abortion double their risk of cervical cancer, compared to non-aborted women, while women with two or more abortions multiply their risk by nearly five times. Similar elevated risks of ovarian and liver cancer have also been linked to single and multiple abortions.[18]

After extensive research, Dr. Joel Brind, professor of endocrinology at City University of New York, concluded, "The single most avoidable risk factor for breast cancer is induced abortion."[19] A woman who has an abortion increases her risk of breast cancer by a minimum of 50 percent and as much as 300 percent.[20]

Some women are unable to conceive after having abortions. Abortion increases the risk of malformations of later children.[21] The frequency of early death for infants born after their mothers have had abortions is between two and four times the normal rate.[22]

## COMMON PSYCHOLOGICAL COMPLICATIONS

Dozens of studies tie abortion to a rise in sexual dysfunction, aversion to sex, loss of intimacy, unexpected guilt, extramarital affairs, traumatic stress syndrome, personality fragmentation, grief response, child abuse and neglect, and increase in alcohol and drug abuse.[23] An Elliot Institute study indicates that women who abort are five times more likely to abuse drugs.[24]

Postabortion specialist David Reardon writes, "In a

study of postabortion patients only eight weeks after their abortion, researchers found that 44 percent complained of nervous disorders, 36 percent had experienced sleep disturbances, 31 percent had regrets about their decision, and 11 percent had been prescribed psychotropic medicine by their family doctor."[25] This is particularly significant since some women show no apparent effects from their abortions until years later.

Women Exploited by Abortion (WEBA) has had over thirty thousand members in more than two hundred chapters across the United States, with chapters in Canada, Germany, Ireland, Japan, Australia, New Zealand, and Africa.[26] Other postabortion support and recovery groups include Victims of Choice, Postabortion Counseling and Education (PACE), Helping and Educating in Abortion-Related Trauma (HEART), Healing Visions Network, Counseling for Abortion-Related Experiences (CARE), Women of Ramah, Project Rachel, Open Arms, Abortion Trauma Services, American Victims of Abortion, and Former Women of Choice. The existence of such groups testifies to the mental and emotional trauma of countless women who have had abortions.

I read a newspaper editorial arguing that abortion is just another surgery, no different from a root canal or appendectomy. But why don't people remember the anniversary of their appendectomy twenty years later? Why don't they find themselves weeping uncontrollably, grieving the loss of their appendix? And where are all the support groups and counseling for those who've had root canals?

(Many men have also suffered trauma due to their involvement in abortion decisions, and the loss of their children.[27] Support groups exist for them as well.[28])

## DEATH FROM LEGAL ABORTIONS

A study of pregnancy-associated deaths published in the *American Journal of Obstetrics and Gynecology* demonstrates that the mortality rate associated with abortion is 2.95 times higher than that of pregnancies carried to term.[29]

The Centers for Disease Control reported ten abortion-related deaths in 1998,[30] but according to the same report, such statistics are of limited value because not all states require reporting. Indeed, abortion clinics have nothing to gain and much to lose by providing information.[31] What makes abortion-related deaths harder to trace is that the majority of the deaths do not occur during the surgery but afterward. Hence, many secondary reasons are routinely identified as the cause of death:

> Consider the mother who hemorrhaged, was transfused, got hepatitis, and died months later. Official cause of death? Hepatitis. Actual cause? Abortion. A perforated uterus leads to pelvic abscess, sepsis (blood poisoning), and death. The official report of the cause of death may list pelvic

abscess and septicemia. Abortion will not be listed. Abortion causes tubal pathology. She has an ectopic pregnancy years later and dies. The cause listed will be ectopic pregnancy. The actual cause? Abortion.[32]

A study published in the *Southern Medical Journal* indicated that "women who have abortions are at significantly higher risk of death than women who give birth."[33] This included a 154 percent higher risk of death from suicide, as well as higher rates of death from accidents and homicides.

*Women's Health After Abortion* is an encyclopedic work citing over five hundred medical journal articles, demonstrating the adverse effects of abortion on women.[34] Anyone still doubting that abortion causes serious long-term harm to women should examine this compelling evidence.

## WHAT WOMEN SAY

In surveys of women who experienced postabortion complications:

1. Over 90 percent said they weren't given enough information to make an informed choice.

2. Over 80 percent said it was very unlikely they would have aborted if they had not been so

strongly encouraged to abort by others, including their abortion counselors.

3. Eighty-three percent said they would have carried to term if they had received support from boyfriends, families, or other important people in their lives.[35]

Every woman deserves better than abortion.

# Chapter 12

# IS ABORTION RIGHT
# WHEN PREGNANCY PRESENTS RISKS
# TO THE MOTHER'S LIFE?

Is abortion justified when a woman's life or health is threatened by pregnancy or childbirth?

It's an extremely rare case when abortion is required to save the mother's life. While he was U.S. Surgeon General, Dr. C. Everett Koop stated that in thirty-six years as a pediatric surgeon, he was never aware of a single situation in which a preborn child's life had to be taken in order to save the mother's life. He said the use of this argument to justify abortion was a "smoke screen." Dr. Landrum Shettles claimed that less than 1 percent of all abortions are performed to save the mother's life.[1]

## SAVE THE LIFE THAT CAN BE SAVED

A woman with toxemia will have adverse health reactions and considerable inconvenience, including probably needing to lie down for much of her pregnancy. This is difficult, but normally not life-threatening. In such cases, abortion for the sake of "health" would not be lifesaving but life-taking.

However, if the mother has a fast-spreading uterine cancer, the surgery to remove the cancer may result in the loss of the child's life. In an ectopic pregnancy the child is developing outside the uterus. He has no hope of survival and may have to be removed to save his mother. These are tragic situations, but even if one life must be lost, the life that can be saved should be. More often than not that life is the mother's. There are rare cases in later stages of pregnancy when the mother can't be saved but the baby can. Again, one life saved is better than two lives lost.

Friends of ours were faced with a situation where removing the mother's life-threatening and rapidly spreading cancer would result in their unborn child's death. The pregnancy was so early that there wasn't time for the child to develop sufficiently to live outside the womb before both mother and child would die. The surgery was performed. But this was in no sense an abortion. The surgery's purpose wasn't to kill the child but to save the mother. The death of the child was a tragic side-effect of lifesaving efforts. This was a consistently pro-life act, since to be pro-life does not mean being pro-life just about babies. It also means being pro-life about women.

Chapter 13

# IS ABORTION RIGHT WHEN PREGNANCY IS DUE TO RAPE OR INCEST?

Studies conducted by the pro-choice Guttmacher Institute indicate that two consenting and fertile adults have only a three percent chance of pregnancy from an act of intercourse. They also indicate there are factors involved in a rape that further reduce these chances for rape victims.[1] The Institute says fourteen thousand[2] abortions per year are due to rape or incest, which amounts to one percent of all abortions.[3] Other studies show that pregnancies due to rape are much rarer, as few as one in a thousand cases.[4] Furthermore, since conception doesn't occur immediately after intercourse, pregnancy can be prevented in many rape cases by removing or washing away the semen before an ovum can be fertilized. (This is very different from using chemicals that can kill an already-conceived child.)

## WHAT'S THE REAL ISSUE?

Where does the misconception come from that many pregnancies are due to rape? Fearful young women sometimes attribute their pregnancies to rape, since doing so avoids condemnation. Norma McCorvey, the young woman called "Roe" in the *Roe v. Wade* case—who elicited sympathy in the court and media because she claimed to be a rape victim—years later admitted she'd lied and hadn't been raped.[5] (McCorvey has since become an outspoken pro-life advocate and has asked the Supreme Court to review and reverse *Roe v. Wade*.[6])

Pro-choice advocates divert attention from the vast majority of abortions by focusing on rape because of its well-deserved sympathy factor. Their frequent references to it leave the false impression that pregnancy due to rape is common, rather than rare.

We have a dear friend who was raped and became pregnant. Because of her circumstances it wasn't best for her to raise the child. She released the baby for adoption into a Christian family. Our friend periodically has contact with the family and her child. It hasn't been easy, and her pain has been great—yet her overwhelming comfort is in knowing her child lives and is loved.

On a television program about abortion, I heard a man say of a child conceived by rape, "Anything of this nature has no rights because it's the product of rape." But how is the nature of this child different from that of any other child? Are some children more worthy to live because their fathers were better people? And why is it that pro-choice advocates are always saying the unborn child is really the mother's, not the father's, until she is raped—

then suddenly the child is viewed as the father's, not the mother's?

The point is not *how* a child was conceived but *that* he was conceived. He is not a despicable "product of rape." He is a unique and wonderful creation of God.

Having and holding an innocent child can do much more good for a victimized woman than the knowledge that an innocent child died in a fruitless attempt to reduce her trauma.

## CONCEIVED BY INCEST

Incest is a horrible crime. Offenders should be punished, and decisive intervention should be taken to remove a girl from the presence of a relative who has sexually abused her. The abuser—*not* the girl or her child—is the problem. Intervention, protection, and ongoing personal help for the girl—not killing an innocent child—is the solution. Despite popular beliefs, fetal deformity is rare in such cases. If the child has handicaps, however, he still deserves to live.

Why should Person A be killed because Person B raped or sexually abused Person A's mother? If your father committed a crime, should you go to jail for it? If you found out today that your biological father had raped your mother, would you feel you no longer had a right to live? A woman who heard me address this issue came up afterward, sobbing. She said, "My mother was raped as a thirteen-year-old. She gave birth to me, then gave me up for adoption. Every time I've heard people say abortion is okay in cases of rape, I've thought, 'Then I guess I have no right to live.'"

Let's punish the rapist and the abuser, not their victims. The woman isn't spoiled goods—she's not "goods" at all but a precious human being with value and dignity that even the vilest act cannot take from her. Likewise, the child isn't a cancer to be removed but a living human being.

## ABORTION COMPOUNDS RAPE TRAUMA

Feminists for Life says, "Some women have reported suffering from the trauma of abortion long after the rape trauma has faded."[7] It's hard to imagine a worse therapy for a woman who's been raped than the guilt and turmoil of having her child killed. One day she'll understand—and those who advised abortion will not be there to help carry her pain and guilt.

In their book *Victims and Victors*, David Reardon and his associates draw on the testimonies of 192 women who experienced pregnancy as the result of rape or incest, and 55 children who were conceived through sexual assault. It turns out that when victims of violence speak for themselves, their opinion of abortion is nearly unanimous—and the exact opposite of what most would predict:

> Nearly all the women interviewed in this anecdotal survey said they regretted aborting the babies conceived via rape or incest. Of those giving an

opinion, more than 90 percent said they would discourage other victims of sexual violence from having an abortion. On the other hand, among the women profiled in the book who conceived due to rape or incest and carried to term, not one expressed regret about her choice.[8]

There's a parallel between the violence of rape and abortion. Both are done by a more powerful person at the expense of the less powerful.

Abortion doesn't bring healing to a rape victim. Imposing capital punishment on the innocent child of a sex offender does nothing bad to the rapist and nothing good to the woman.

Creating a second victim never undoes the damage to the first.

Section 4

# OTHER IMPORTANT ISSUES

# Chapter 14

# WHAT ABOUT DISABLED AND UNWANTED CHILDREN?

Some argue, "It's cruel to let a handicapped child be born to a miserable and meaningless life." But what do the disabled think about their lives? Spina bifida patients were asked whether their handicaps made life meaningless and if they should have been allowed to die after birth. "Their unanimous response was forceful. Of course they wanted to live! In fact, they thought the question was ridiculous."[1]

I heard a pro-choice advocate say of a severely handicapped child, "Should a woman be forced to bring a monster into the world?" Only by using such words can we deceive ourselves into believing them. The term *vegetable* is another popular word for disadvantaged humans. Such terminology dehumanizes people in our eyes but doesn't change who they are.

A bruised apple is still an apple. A blind dog is still a dog. A senile woman is still a woman. A handicapped child is still a child. A person's nature and worth aren't changed by a handicap.

Some doctors recommend "terminating the pregnancy" if a couple's genetic history suggests a risk of abnormality. The standard test for possible deformities is done by amniocentesis. In 2000, the National Vital Statistics Report indicated that 28.9 women per 1,000 suffered complications from amniocentesis, placing the risk factor at nearly three per hundred women.[2] The Centers for Disease Control estimate that in early amniocentesis the rate of death to the unborn through miscarriage is "between one in 400 and one in 200 procedures." The study also found a striking tenfold increase in the risk of clubfoot deformity after early amniocentesis.[3] Ironically, then, a procedure designed to identify fetal deformity actually has a considerable chance of causing it.

Amniocentesis is frequently done to identify Down's syndrome children so parents have the option of abortion. The risk of miscarriage as a result of amniocentesis is almost exactly the same as the risk for Down's syndrome.[4]

## SOCIETY'S SCHIZOPHRENIA

A survey of pediatricians and pediatric surgeons revealed that more than two out of three would go along with parents' wishes to deny lifesaving surgery to a child with Down's syndrome. On the one hand, we provide special parking and elevators for the handicapped. We talk tenderly about those poster children with spina bifida and Down's syndrome. We sponsor the Special Olympics and cheer on the competitors, speaking of the joy and inspiration they bring us. But when we hear a woman is carrying one of these very children, we say, "Kill it."

Significantly, "there has not been a single organization of parents of mentally retarded children that has ever endorsed abortion."[5]

Suppose your six-year-old becomes blind or paraplegic. He's now a burden. Raising him is expensive, inconvenient, and hard on your mental health. Should you put him to death? If a law were passed that made it legal to put him to death, would you do it? If not, why not?

You wouldn't kill your handicapped child *because you know him*. But killing an unborn child just because you haven't held him in your arms and can't hear his cry doesn't change his value or reduce his loss. Give yourself a chance to know your child. You *will* love him.

What about the anencephalic child who doesn't have a fully developed brain? Since he will die anyway, doctors often advise parents to have an abortion. But it's one thing to know a child will probably die, and entirely another to choose to take his life. Many families have had precious experiences naming, holding, and bonding with an anencephalic baby after birth. When he dies, they experience healthy grief at the natural death of their family member. This is in stark contrast to the unhealthy grief and guilt that comes from denying a baby's place in the family, and taking his life.

The quality of a society is largely defined by how it

treats its weakest members. Killing the innocent is never justified because it relieves others of a burden. It's not a solution to inflict suffering on one person in order to avoid it in another. If we abort children because of their handicaps, it jeopardizes all handicapped people.

## THE BURDEN OF BEING UNWANTED

Planned Parenthood argues that unwanted children "get lower grades, particularly in language skills." It says unwanted adolescents "perform increasingly poorly in school" and are "less likely to excel under increased school pressure." And "they are less than half as likely as wanted children to pursue higher education."[6]

I don't question the accuracy of these findings. They tell us what we should already know—the importance of wanting our children. Instead, however, pro-choice advocates use such research to justify aborting the "unwanted."

There are unwanted pregnancies, but *there is no such thing as an unwanted child*. While certain people may not want them, other people desperately want them.

Nearly 1.3 million American families want to adopt, some so badly that the scarcity of adoptable babies is a source of major depression. There's such a demand for babies that a black market has developed where babies are sold for as much as $50,000. Not just "normal" babies are wanted; many people request special-needs babies, including those with Down's syndrome and spina bifida.[7]

Many children who are at first unwanted by their

mothers are very much wanted later in the pregnancy, and even more at birth. Unfortunately, many women who would have wanted the child by their sixth month of pregnancy get an abortion in their third month.

Furthermore, many children wanted at birth are *not* wanted when they are crying at 2:00 A.M. six weeks later. Shall whether or not the parents want the baby still determine whether she deserves to live? If that's a legitimate standard before birth, why not after?

The problem of unwantedness is a good argument for wanting children. But it's a poor argument for killing them.

One of the most misleading aspects of pro-choice argumentation is making it appear that abortion is in the best interests of the baby. This is so absurd as to be laughable, were it not so tragic. A little person is torn limb from limb, for *her* benefit? Similarly, slave owners argued that slavery was in the best interest of blacks. (Who are we kidding?)

People say, "I can't have this child because I can't give it a good life." And what is their solution to not being able to give him a good life? To take from him the only life he has.

## EVERY CHILD A WANTED CHILD

*Unwanted* describes not the child but an attitude of some adults toward the child. The real problem isn't unwanted children, but unwanting adults.

"Wanting" is simply one person's subjective and changeable feeling toward another. The "unwanted" child is a real person regardless of anyone else's feelings toward her. A woman's worth was once judged by whether or not a man wanted her. A child's worth is now judged by whether or not her mother wants her. Both of these are tragic injustices. Planned Parenthood's slogan, "Every child a wanted child," is something we should all agree with. Where we disagree is in the proper way to finish the sentence. How do *you* think the sentence should be finished?

- Every child a wanted child, so…let's place children in homes where they are wanted, and let's learn to want children more.
- Every child a wanted child, so…let's identify unwanted children before they're born and kill them by abortion.

Everyone agrees that children should be wanted. The only question is this: Should we get rid of the *unwanting* or get rid of the *children*?

When it comes to the unborn, the abortion rights position is more accurately reflected in a different slogan, one that doesn't look so good on a bumper sticker: "Every unwanted child a dead child."

## Chapter 15

# DOES ABORTION
# PREVENT CHILD ABUSE?

Ateenage girl delivered a child in a Delaware motel. She and her boyfriend put the baby, still alive, in a plastic bag and dropped it in a Dumpster. A seventeen-year-old mother who was attending night school hurled her baby into the river after she couldn't find a babysitter. Similar stories abound.

In 1973, when abortion was first legalized, United States child abuse cases were estimated at 167,000 annually.[1] According to the U.S. Department of Health and Human Services, approximately 903,000 children were victims of abuse during 2001, a number more than five times greater.[2]

The increase in child abuse is even more dramatic, since the 45 million American children killed by surgical abortions (and an unknown number by chemical abortions) aren't counted as victims of child abuse. Yet abortion is the earliest child abuse, and no other is more deadly. The argument that aborting a child prevents child abuse is true only in the same sense that killing a wife prevents wife abuse. Dead people can no longer be abused…but preventing their abuse by killing them is convoluted logic.

Why have children been abused far more since abortion was legalized? Because *abortion has changed the way we think about children.*

## WHAT THE STUDIES SHOW

"Having more unwanted children results in more child abuse," pro-choicers argue. Studies, however, disagree.

University of Southern California professor Edward Lenoski conducted a landmark study of 674 abused children. He discovered that 91 percent of the parents admitted they wanted the child they had abused.[3] The pro-choice argument that it is unwanted children who are destined for abuse may sound logical, but the best study done to date demonstrates it is false.

"Studies indicate that child abuse is more frequent among mothers who have previously had an abortion."[4] Dr. Philip Ney's studies indicate that this is partially due to the guilt and depression caused by abortion, which hinders the mother's ability to bond with future children.[5] He documents that having an abortion decreases a parent's natural restraint against feelings of rage toward small children.[6]

Both mother and father override their natural impulse to care for a helpless child when they choose abortion. Having suppressed that preserving instinct, it may become less effective in holding back rage against a newborn's helplessness, a toddler's crying, or a pre-schooler's defiance.[7]

The attitude that results in abortion is exactly the same attitude that results in child abuse. Furthermore, if she doesn't abort, the mother can look at her difficult three-year-old and think, "I had the right to abort you." The child owes her everything; she owes the child nothing. This causes resentment of demands requiring parental sacrifice. Even if subconscious, the logic is inescapable: If it was all right to kill the same child before birth, surely it's all right to slap him around now.

Of the five thousand American children murdered every year (the figure doesn't include abortions), 95 percent are killed by one or both of their parents.[8] There's a pervasive notion that children belong to their parents. Adults think they have the same right to dispose of their children that society assured them they had before the children were born. Once the child-abuse mentality grips a society, it doesn't restrict itself to only one age group. If preborn children aren't safe, no children are safe.

Peter Singer says,

> There [is a] lack of any clear boundary between the newborn infant, who is clearly not a person in the ethically relevant sense, and the young child who is. In our book, *Should the Baby Live?*, my colleague Helga Kuhse and I suggested that a period of twenty-eight days after birth might be

allowed before an infant is accepted as having the same right to life as others.[9]

Children granted a right to life at twenty-eight days after birth? Why not wait until six months? Or six years? Killing a five-, ten-, or fifteen-year-old child is really just a postnatal abortion, isn't it? As Singer has demonstrated, once you establish it's all right to kill a person, logically the door is wide open to killing the same person at a variety of ages, for a variety of reasons.

The solution to battered children outside the womb is not battered children inside the womb. The solution to child abuse isn't doing the abusing *earlier*. It's not doing it at all.

## Chapter 16

# PERSONALLY OPPOSED TO ABORTION, BUT PRO-CHOICE?

Many people say, "I'm not pro-abortion, but I'm pro-choice."

But how would you respond to someone who said, "I'm not pro-rape, I'm just pro-choice about rape"? You'd realize his position implies that rape doesn't really hurt anyone, and that it's sometimes justifiable. You'd say, "To be pro-choice about rape *is* to be pro-rape."

In exactly the same way, to be pro-choice about abortion is to be pro-abortion.

At first glance the bumper sticker slogan makes sense: "Against Abortion? Don't Have One." The logic applies perfectly to flying planes, playing football, or eating pizza…but not to rape, torture, kidnapping, or murder.

## A MIDDLE POSITION?

Some imagine that being personally opposed to abortion, while believing others have the right to choose it, is some kind of compromise between the pro-abortion and pro-life positions. It isn't. Pro-choice people vote the same as pro-abortion people. To the baby who dies it makes no difference whether those who refused to protect her were pro-abortion or "merely" pro-choice about abortion.

The only good reason to oppose abortion is a reason that compels us to oppose *others* doing it—it's child killing. Being personally against abortion but favoring another's right to abortion is self-contradictory. It's exactly like saying, "I'm personally against child abuse, but I defend my neighbor's right to abuse his child if that is his choice." Or "I'm personally against slave-owning, but if others want to own slaves that's none of my business." Or, "I'm not personally in favor of wife-beating, but I don't want to impose my morality on others, so I'm pro-choice about wife-beating."

A radio talk show host told me she was offended that some people called her "pro-abortion" instead of "pro-choice." I asked her, on the air, "Why don't you want to be called pro-abortion? Is there something wrong with abortion?" She responded, "Abortion is tough. It's not like anybody really wants one." I said, "I don't get it. What makes it tough? Why wouldn't someone want an abortion?" She said, suddenly impassioned, "Well, you know, it's a tough thing to kill your baby!"

The second she said it, she caught herself, but it was too late. In an unguarded moment she'd revealed what she knew, what *everyone* knows if they'll only admit it: *Abortion is difficult for the same reason it's wrong*—because it's killing a child.

And there's no reason good enough for killing a child.

## Chapter 17

# WHAT ABOUT ADOPTION?

O ne of the great ironies of the pro-choice movement is that it has fostered the idea that women have no choice but abortion. The pro-choice movement could just as well be called the no-choice-but-abortion movement. Many women will testify that for them "pro-choice" really meant "no choice."

Fathers, mothers, boyfriends, husbands, teachers, school counselors, doctors, nurses, media, and peers often pressure the pregnant woman into making the one choice her conscience tells her is wrong, a choice that is more other people's than her own. (But where will *they* be when she realizes what she's done?)

Do women really want abortions? Frederica Mathewes-Green, past president of Feminists for Life, says, "No one wants an abortion as she wants an ice-cream cone or a Porsche. She wants an abortion as an animal, caught in a trap, wants to gnaw off its own leg. Abortion is a tragic attempt to escape a desperate situation by an act of violence and self-loss."[1]

Abortion isn't a free choice as much as a last resort. Most women would choose not to abort if they felt they would get the emotional and financial support they need.

Nearly two-thirds of aborted women describe themselves as "forced into abortion because of their particular circumstances...over 84 percent state that they would have kept their babies under better circumstances."[2]

## THE ALTERNATIVE THAT'S RARELY MENTIONED

The National Council for Adoption estimates 1.3 million couples are waiting to adopt a child.[3] Yet each year, while 1.3 million children are being killed by abortion, less than 50,000 new children are made available for adoption. This means that for every new adoptable child, thirty others are killed. For every couple that adopts, another forty wait in line.[4]

In a society that values choice, why aren't doctors, schools, family planning clinics, and abortion clinics required to present women with facts about *all* available choices, including adoption? A friend told us, "When I was an abortion clinic counselor, I was totally uninformed of abortion alternatives. I never recommended adoption or keeping the child. I was completely unaware of the medical facts, including the development of the fetus. I received no training in factual matters—my job was just to make sure women went through with their abortions."

With this kind of "counseling," how many women will choose anything other than abortion? Former owners and employees of abortion clinics have stated it was their job to "sell abortions" to pregnant women. Some clinics even hire professional marketing experts to train their staff in abortion sales.[5]

Adoption is a positive alternative that avoids the responsibility of child raising, while saving a life and making a family happy. It's tragic that adoption is so infrequently chosen…or even offered as an alternative to abortion.

Research with pregnancy care centers indicates emotional resistance to adoption is the most common barrier that surfaces among abortion-bound women.[6] The reason that adoption may be painful is the same reason that abortion is devastating—a human life is involved.

Adoption is often portrayed negatively in pro-choice literature. Pro-choice advocates Carole Anderson and Lee Campbell say of adoption, "The unnecessary separation of mothers and children is a cruel, but regrettably usual, punishment that can last a lifetime."[7]

While calling adoption cruel, they fail to mention a woman's lifelong guilt when she realizes she's killed her child. Adoption is hardly a punishment to a woman who feels she can't raise her child. Tough though it may feel, it's a heaven-sent alternative.

There are many excellent on-line adoption resources,[8] as well as the comprehensive *Encyclopedia of Adoption,* with over four hundred informative articles about every aspect of adoption.[9] We owe it to both women and children to be informed about adoption.

## ABORTION ROBS FAMILIES WAITING TO ADOPT

By carrying a child to term, a young woman accepts responsibility for her choices. She grows and matures. She can look back with pride and satisfaction that she did the right thing by allowing her child both life and a good family. Of course, adoption is only one alternative. The young woman may choose to keep the baby and raise him herself. Either choice can be right.

"What kind of mother would I be to give up a child for adoption?" some ask. The irony is that a mother who wouldn't give away her child because he's too precious will instead kill that same child. The question she should ask isn't "How could I give up my baby for adoption?" but "How could I kill my baby by abortion?" Even if she cannot care for her child herself, can't she see that she should let others love and care for him? Unfortunately, it's not so simple.

The woman wants her crisis to end, yet adoption appears to leave the situation unresolved "with uncertainty and guilt as far as she can see for both herself and her child."[10] She may feel like she would be not only a mother, but a bad mother, who gave her child away to strangers. She may worry that she'd be abandoning the child or that the child will be abused. The logic here is based on her wishful thinking that if she aborts, the child will not be a child and she will not have been a mother. In reality, of course, she cannot choose whether or not to become a mother or whether or not her child is real—both of these are unalterable facts. Her child *is* real, and therefore she *is* a mother. The only question is, what will she, the mother, do with her child?

Because she hasn't yet bonded with her child, abortion may seem an easy solution, while parting with her child after birth would be emotionally difficult. But the child's life is just as real before bonding as after. The woman has three choices: have her child and raise him, have her child and allow another family to raise him, or kill her child. Though abortion often seems most attractive, ultimately it's most destructive.

We must help young women to see child raising, adoption, and abortion as they really are. We should portray adoption as a courageous choice, one that will give life to a child and to a family.

The pregnant teenager we took into our home had two abortions, but while with us she gave birth to her baby and released him for adoption. It wasn't easy, but this wonderful woman, years later, told me: "I look back at the three babies I no longer have, but with very different feelings. The two I aborted fill me with grief and regret. But when I think of the one I gave up for adoption, I'm filled with joy, because I know he's being raised by a family that wanted him."

The Christian community should make a concerted effort to overcome the negative spin on adoption. We should speak of it positively and show high regard for young women who release their children for adoption. We should publicly honor adoptive parents and bless adopted children. We should make prominent the excellent resources on adoption and celebrate adoption in our churches. Only by doing so can we help young women realize adoption is the courageous choice and one that both they and their child will later be profoundly thankful for.

Pro-choice ends up meaning no choice or poor choice. But adoption offers a choice that's wise, compassionate, and in *everyone's* best interests.

# SPIRITUAL
# PERSPECTIVES AND
# OPPORTUNITIES

## Chapter 18

# CAN GOD FORGIVE ABORTIONS?

Millions of women and men, both in society and in the church, are suffering under the guilt of abortion. As we saw in chapter 1, two-thirds of those getting abortions identify themselves as Protestants or Catholics. Nearly one out of five women getting an abortion identifies herself as an evangelical Christian.[1] Many of the fathers of these children are also part of our churches.

If you're a woman who's had an abortion, or advised another to have one, this chapter is for you. If you're a man who's been involved in an abortion decision—whether it concerned your girlfriend, wife, daughter, or anyone—it's also for you.

It's counterproductive to try to eliminate guilt feelings without dealing with guilt's cause. Others may say, "You have nothing to feel guilty about," but you know better. Only by denying reality can you avoid guilt feelings. Denial sets you up for emotional collapse whenever something reminds you of the child you once carried. You need a permanent solution to your guilt problem, a solution based on reality, not pretense.

Because the Bible offers that solution, I will quote from

it. Ask your church leader, women's group leader, or a Christian friend or family member to help you understand.

## THE WORK OF CHRIST

The good news is that God loves you and desires to forgive you for your abortion, whether or not you knew what you were doing. But before the good news can be appreciated, we must know the bad news. The bad news is there's true moral guilt, and all of us are guilty of many moral offenses against God, of which abortion is only one. "All have sinned and fall short of the glory of God" (Romans 3:23).

Sin is falling short of God's holy standards. It separates us from a relationship with God (Isaiah 59:2). Sin deceives us, making us think that wrong is right and right is wrong (Proverbs 14:12). "The wages of sin is death, but the gift of God is eternal life in Christ Jesus our Lord" (Romans 6:23).

Jesus Christ, God's Son, loved us so much that He became a member of the human race to deliver us from our sin problem (John 3:16). He identified with us in our weakness, without being tainted by our sin (Hebrews 2:17–18; 4:15–16). Jesus died on the cross as the only one worthy to pay the penalty for our sins demanded by God's holiness (2 Corinthians 5:21). He rose from the grave, defeating sin and conquering death (1 Corinthians 15:3–4, 54–57).

When Christ died on the cross for us, He said, "It is finished" (John 19:30). The Greek word translated "it is finished" was written across certificates of debt when they were canceled. It meant "paid in full." Christ died to fully pay our debt.

## FULL FORGIVENESS

Because of Christ's work on the cross on our behalf, God freely offers us forgiveness. Here are just a few of those offers:

> He does not treat us as our sins deserve
>   or repay us according to our iniquities.
> As far as the east is from the west,
>   so far has he removed our transgressions from us.
> As a father has compassion on his children,
>   so the LORD has compassion on those who fear
>   him.
> (Psalm 103:10, 12–13)

> If we confess our sins, he is faithful and just and will forgive us our sins and purify us from all unrighteousness. (1 John 1:9)

> Therefore, there is now no condemnation for those who are in Christ Jesus. (Romans 8:1)

## A GIFT THAT CAN'T BE EARNED

Salvation is a gift—"For it is by grace you have been saved, through faith—and this not from yourselves, it is the gift of God—not by works, so that no one can boast"

(Ephesians 2:8–9). This gift cannot be worked for, earned, or achieved. It's not dependent on our merit or effort, but solely on Christ's sacrifice for us.

God offers us the gift of forgiveness and eternal life, but it's not automatically ours. In order to have the gift, we must choose to accept it.

You may think, "But I don't deserve forgiveness after all I've done." That's exactly right. None of us deserves forgiveness. If we deserved it, we wouldn't need it. That's the point of grace. Christ got what we deserved on the cross, so we could get what we don't deserve—a clean slate, a fresh start.

Once forgiven, we can look forward to spending eternity with Christ and our spiritual family (John 14:1–3; Revelation 20:11–22:6). You can look forward to being reunited in heaven with your loved ones covered by Christ's blood (1 Thessalonians 4:13–18).

## No Need to Dwell on Past Sins

A promiscuous woman wept at Christ's feet, kissed them, and wiped them with her hair. Jesus said to a judgmental bystander, "Therefore, I tell you, her many sins have been forgiven—for she loved much" (Luke 7:47). Jesus offers the same forgiveness to all of us.

God doesn't want you to go through life punishing yourself for your abortion or for any other wrong you've done. Your part is to accept Christ's atonement, not to repeat it. Jesus said to an immoral woman, "Your sins are forgiven…. Your faith has saved you; go in peace" (Luke 7:48, 50). Women rejected by society came to Jesus, and He welcomed them with compassion and forgiveness.

No matter what you've done, no sin is beyond the reach of God's grace. He has seen us at our worst and still loves us. There are no limits to His forgiving grace. And there is no freedom like the freedom of forgiveness.

You may feel immediately cleansed when you confess your sins, or you may need help working through it. Either way, you're forgiven. You should try to forget what lies behind and move on to a positive future made possible by Christ (Philippians 3:13–14). Whenever we start feeling unforgiven, it's time to go back to the Bible and remind ourselves, and each other, of God's forgiveness.

Joining a group for postabortion healing can help you immensely. There are postabortion Bible studies designed for women, and others for men. Many on-line resources can help you find the support group you need.[2]

## FORGIVENESS FOLLOWED BY RIGHT CHOICES

Many women who've had abortions carry understandable bitterness toward men who used and abused them, toward parents who pressured them, and toward those who mis-led them into a choice that resulted in their child's death. God expects us to take the forgiveness He's given us and extend it to others (Matthew 6:14–15).

You need to become part of a therapeutic community, a family of Christians called a church. (If you're already in a church, share your abortion experience with someone to get the specific help you need.) You may feel self-conscious around Christians because of your past. You shouldn't. A true Christ-centered church isn't a showcase for saints but a hospital for sinners. You won't be judged and condemned for sins Christ has forgiven. The people you're joining are just as human and just as imperfect as you. Most church people aren't self-righteous. Those who are should be pitied because they don't understand God's grace.

A good church will teach the truths of the Bible, and will provide love, acceptance, and support for you. If you cannot find such a church in your area, contact our organization at the address in the back of this book and we'll gladly help you.

A healthy step you can take is to reach out to women experiencing unwelcome pregnancies. God can eventually use your experience to equip you to help others and to share with them God's love. My wife and I have a number of good friends who've had abortions. Through their caring pro-life efforts they've given to other women the help they wish someone had given them. Telling their stories has not only saved children's lives, and saved mothers from the pain of abortion, but has helped bring healing to them. It can do the same for you.

## Chapter 19

# PRO-LIFE ISSUES:
# DISTRACTION FROM THE GREAT
# COMMISSION OR PART OF IT?

Many well-meaning Christians believe that churches shouldn't mention abortion. Some say that by talking about abortion we'll make people feel guilty. But the reason for talking about it is to *prevent* abortion and the guilt it brings, and to offer help and hope to those who are guilt-ridden and need to be free. That our churches are filled with people who've been involved with abortion is a poor reason for keeping silent about it. In fact, it's the best argument for addressing the issue head-on, and offering all the perspective, help, and support we can.

A seminary student at my church told me something I've often heard in one form or another: "Issues like abortion are just a distraction from the main thing."

"What's the main thing?" I asked.

"The Great Commission," he said. "Winning people to Christ. That's what we're supposed to do. Everything else is a distraction."

He was referring to Christ's words in Matthew 28:19–20: "Therefore go and make disciples of all nations, baptizing them in the name of the Father and of the Son and of the Holy Spirit, and teaching them to obey everything I have commanded you."

Was he right? Is pro-life action a distraction from the Great Commission…or is it part of it?

## A MAN NAMED WILLIAM

Two hundred years ago there lived an Englishman named William, an outspoken slavery opponent who boycotted sugar from the West Indies because it was the product of slavery. William sensed God wanted him to go to India, where he was shocked to discover that many Hindus exposed their infant children to die. They also abandoned the weak, sick, and lepers. The British government in India looked the other way because it didn't want to interfere with the culture or religion, but William felt compelled to interfere because people were dying.

One day William witnessed the practice called *sati*, where widows were burned alive on the funeral pyre of their deceased husband. After seeing one such death, he stood up in front of a group assembled to burn a woman alive and told them the practice was wrong. He led a group of missionaries in protest. He set up public debates on the subject to bring God's perspective to light.

On Sunday morning, December 6, 1829, after years of activism, William received the official decree forbidding widow burning. He was scheduled to preach in church that morning but he didn't. Instead, he dedicated the whole day to translating the decree into the Bengali language, because he knew that lives hung in the balance.

Some criticized William for his moral and political actions. They said, "That's not what you're here for. That's not your calling. Focus on the main thing. Just preach the gospel and pray."

Who was this social activist so concerned about morality and laws and saving human lives? His name was William Carey, known today as "the Father of Modern Missions." When we think of the Great Commission and the modern missions movement, no other name is as prominent as his.

Carey went to India to win people to Christ and disciple them, not just by sharing the gospel, but by living it— which included intervening to save lives and laboring to change public opinion and evil laws.

## FOOTSTEPS TO FOLLOW IN

John Wesley actively opposed slavery. Charles Finney had a major role in the illegal Underground Railroad, saving the lives of many slaves, while being criticized by fellow Christians because of his civil disobedience. D. L. Moody opened homes for underprivileged girls, rescuing them from exploitation. Charles Spurgeon built homes to help care for elderly women and to rescue orphans from the streets of London. Amy Carmichael intervened for the sexually exploited girls of India, rescuing them from temple prostitution. She built them homes, a school, and a hospital.

All of these Christians are known as missionaries and evangelists, people who carried out the Great Commission. Yet we rarely pay attention to their radical commitment to personal and social intervention for the weak, needy, and exploited.

Perhaps their evangelism was effective because they lived out the gospel that they preached. There is no conflict between the gospel and social concern and personal intervention for the needy. In fact, there is a direct connection between them.

## PART OF THE "MAIN THING"

We should try to save lives for the simple reason that the Bible our churches preach from every week says we should:

> Rescue those being led away to death. (Proverbs 24:11)

> Defend the cause of the weak and fatherless; maintain the rights of the poor and oppressed. (Psalm 82:3)

> Love your neighbor as yourself. (Matthew 19:19)

God's people are to give special care to women without husbands and children without fathers (James 1:27). Who qualifies more for this care than an unmarried woman and her unborn child?

In Luke 10:25 we read of the lawyer who asked, "What must I do to inherit eternal life?" Jesus answered, "'Love the Lord your God'…and 'Love your neighbor as yourself'" (v. 27). Jesus called loving God the first and greatest commandment, and loving your neighbor the second greatest (Matthew 22:37–39). So the Great Commission, by itself, isn't the greatest commandment…rather, it's part of loving God and loving your neighbor.

Nothing opens doors for evangelism like need-meeting ministries. Students who do a speech on abortion have follow-up conversations that can lead to sharing the gospel. Those who work at pregnancy centers have great opportunities to share Christ, as do those who pass out literature at abortion clinics and go on campuses to educate about abortion. People who open their homes to pregnant women demonstrate a love which leads to sharing the gospel. Whenever we meet people's needs, evangelism becomes both natural and credible.

## THREE PERSPECTIVES
## ON THE GREAT COMMISSION

We need to consider three perspectives to understand the relationship between pro-life efforts and the Great Commission.

First, the Great Commission is a central command, but Jesus labeled another command the greatest. The Great

Commission is really just an extension of the command to love God and our neighbors.

Second, even if all there was to the Great Commission was evangelism, standing up for those whose lives are endangered would qualify because it opens significant doors for evangelism.

Third, in His Great Commission, Jesus didn't tell us only to evangelize. He told us to be "teaching them to obey everything I have commanded you" (Matthew 28:20). He didn't just say teaching them to *believe;* He said teaching them to *obey.*

Jesus commands us to have compassion and to take sacrificial action for the weak and needy. So that's part of "everything I have commanded you." And if we fail to obey that part, and fail to teach others to obey it, we are not fulfilling the Great Commission.

If the church doesn't intervene for unborn children and their mothers, and if we don't teach our people to help them, then we fail to fulfill the Great Commission.

Churches are to be the backbone of God's work for the needy. If your church isn't doing enough for the unborn and their mothers, then perhaps God is calling you to step forward and help your church and its leaders take on this vital ministry.

Chapter 20

# HOW CAN I HELP UNBORN BABIES
# AND THEIR MOTHERS?

There are many excellent pro-life organizations across the country and around the world. They specialize in a wide variety of activities that include abstinence education, fetal development education, counseling pregnant women, influencing legislation, offering adoptions, confronting our culture about the prenatal holocaust, picketing abortion clinics, disseminating scientific and psychological studies, prayer, sidewalk counseling outside abortion clinics, and helping post-aborted women and men. There are trained consultants offering counseling and answering toll-free phone calls and e-mail twenty-four hours a day.[1]

## A PLEA FOR PRO-LIFE UNITY

Over the last twenty years I've had the privilege of working with and observing a wide variety of pro-life ministries. I've seen the great strengths in different approaches, which reach different audiences and attract different volunteers and supporters.

Pro-lifers, understandably passionate about their

cause, sometimes assume that their form of pro-life ministry is the most important way, the right way, or even the *only* way. This is as shortsighted as it would be for a soldier to say the Navy's not on the cutting edge, or for a sailor to say Army Rangers aren't doing important work, and they should all be Navy SEALs instead. The pro-life task is huge and multifaceted, calling for multiple strategies. We should *not* all be trying to do the same thing.

We're commanded, "All of you, live in harmony with one another; be sympathetic, love as brothers, be compassionate and humble" (1 Peter 3:8). Humble minds and tender hearts are quick to learn from others with different personalities, gifts, passions, and strategies. We need gentleness, patience, love, peace, and unity in God's Spirit (Ephesians 4:1–6).

For years I led a bimonthly meeting of pro-life leaders from a wide spectrum of groups. We got to know, understand, and learn from each other. We found activities we could cooperate in, and discovered we'd been trying to reinvent the wheel in creating materials and programs other groups already had in place. Many commented to me that they'd never understood some of the other groups and had been suspicious of their approach. They'd even felt competitive. But as they got to know these people, they saw their hearts and understood their goals. They came to love and appreciate their brothers and sisters God had called to different aspects of pro-life ministry.

Look for the best organizations to fit your background,

personality, gifting, and sense of God's calling. Contact information is available for a wide variety of fine pro-life organizations, national and regional and local.[2] If you need help finding a pro-life group in your area, contact our office for assistance.[3]

## What You Can Do

If you're part of a Christ-centered, Bible-teaching church, contact your leaders and ask about pro-life ministry in your church and community. (If you're not part of such a church, find one.) We must resist the notion that "I'm just one person, we're just one small church, we can't make a difference." You can't eliminate need, but you can be used of God to meet needs in exciting ways. How do you help millions of needy people? One at a time.

The following are not things everyone should do, but merely a menu from which to choose what best suits your gifts and your resources:

*1. Open your home.* Help a pregnant girl or welcome an "unwanted" child for foster care or adoption. Or devote one day a week to watching the children of single mothers.

*2. Volunteer your time, talents, and services.* Give personal care to pregnant women, newborns, drug babies, orphans, the handicapped, the elderly, street people, and others in need. Donate time, equipment, furniture, clothes, professional skills, and money to pregnancy centers, adoption ministries, women's homes, abstinence agencies, and right-to-life educational and political organizations and other pro-life groups. Mow their lawn, do their cleaning or plumbing, design them a Web site, fix their computers.

*3. Be an initiator.* If there's not a pro-life ministry nearby, consider starting one. Build a coalition. Consider renting space next to an abortion clinic or Planned Parenthood office. Establish a pregnancy counseling clinic or pro-life information center. Develop a beautiful memorial to the unborn, perhaps in the form of a rose garden, on your church property or in your community.[4]

*4. Become thoroughly informed.* Know the facts so you can rehearse in advance the best responses to the pro-choice arguments.[5] Many fine books, tapes, and videos are available, as well as excellent (and usually free) pro-life newsletters. There are many outstanding pro-life websites.[6] While surgical abortions have begun to decrease, chemical abortions are increasing. Become informed about chemicals, including RU-486, the abortion pill. Investigate Norplant, Depo-Provera, the Mini-Pill, and even the birth control pill—while these are primarily contraceptives, they sometimes permit conception, but may prevent the newly conceived person from implanting in the endometrium, thereby causing early abortions.[7] Become informed enough to draw your own conclusions.

*5. Talk to your friends, neighbors, and coworkers.* Graciously challenge others to rethink their assumptions. Give them a copy of this book, with some pages marked for their attention. Study the issues in more detail in my larger book *ProLife Answers to ProChoice Arguments*. Give away novels with a pro-life theme, such as *The Atonement Child* by Francine Rivers, *Tears in a Bottle* by Sylvia Bambola, and my book *Deadline*.

*6. Promote discussions of abortion.* Go to Internet chat rooms, bringing pro-life perspectives. Consider establishing your own pro-life website. Call in and speak up on talk shows, and ask for equal time on television and radio stations that present the pro-choice position. Order and distribute pro-life literature. Speak up so the pro-choice bandwagon doesn't go unchallenged. As I state in my book *The Grace and Truth Paradox,* it's vitally important that we approach subjects such as abortion in a Christlike manner. Jesus came full of grace and truth (John 1:14). If people are to see Jesus in us, we must offer the truth with grace.

*7. Write letters.* Be courteous, concise, accurate, and memorable. Quote brief references cited in this book and the larger *ProLife Answers*. Letters to the editor in a national magazine or larger newspaper may be read by hundreds of thousands.

*8. Encourage business boycotts of abortion clinics.* Contact influential people, including landlords, businesses, insurance providers, medical providers, and various service providers, graciously stating that you cannot in good conscience patronize those who lend their services to the killing of children.

*9. Be active in the political process.* Meet with your representatives and share your views on abortion. Draft, circulate, and sign petitions for pro-life ballot measures. Run for political office, school board, or precinct chairman. Stand by pro-life candidates with your time and money. Vote.

*10. Join or organize a pro-life task force in your church.* Ask your leaders for guidance. Give them literature, ask them to watch a video. Recruit positive people who are supportive of the church's other ministries to help you formulate and implement a plan of education and mobilization. Request periodic special offerings for pro-life ministries. Provide bulletin inserts and literature for your church to distribute during Sanctity of Human Life week in January.[8] Acquire *Why ProLife?* at bulk rates and distribute a copy to everyone in your church. (All royalties from this book go to pro-life ministries; none go to the author.) If your church leaders want ideas for preparing their messages, offer to provide them with some of the many fine resources available.[9]

*11. Utilize excellent pro-life resources.* Show in church services or classes pro-life videos such as "Life Is Sacred."[10] Consider showing a video that depicts abortions.[11] (Prepare people and warn in advance it's not for children.) Distribute contact information for a variety of pro-life groups in your community. Place a bench ad or a billboard with an 800 number for pregnant women to call. Start a group for sidewalk counselors; plan a prayer vigil or a protest. Contact the pro-life groups in your area. They know a lot you don't, and they'll be glad to serve as a resource.

*12. Pray daily for pro-life ministries, churches, church leaders, mothers, and babies.* Organize your own prayer group. If the darkness of child-killing is to be overcome with the light of truth and compassion, it will require spiritual warfare, fought with humble and persistent prayer (Ephesians 6:10–20).

*13. Give to pro-life organizations.* I've seen close-up a wide variety of pro-life ministries. In nearly every case I've walked away impressed with the difference that's being made. I encourage you and your church to find a few pro-life organizations in your area, or one of the national or international pro-life ministries, and give generously to them.

Ask yourself, *Five minutes after I die, what will I wish I would have given on behalf of the helpless while I still had the chance?* Why not spend the rest of our lives closing the gap between what we'll wish we would have given and what we *are* giving?

We have a brief opportunity—a lifetime on earth—to use our resources to make a difference for eternity. Picture the moment in heaven, and think how you'll feel when someone approaches you, smiling broadly, and says, "Thank you! Your gifts helped save my life...and my child's."

# ABOUT THE AUTHOR

R andy Alcorn is a researcher and bestselling author of twenty books. His nonfiction includes *The Grace and Truth Paradox*, *The Treasure Principle*, and *ProLife Answers to ProChoice Arguments*. His novels include *Deadline*, *Dominion*, *The Ishbane Conspiracy* and the Gold Medallion winner *Safely Home*. The father of two married daughters, Karina Franklin and Angela Stump, Randy lives in Gresham, Oregon, with his wife, Nanci, who is also his best friend. The author's organization is Eternal Perspective Ministries, which can be contacted through www.epm.org, 503-663-6481, or 2229 East Burnside #23, Gresham, OR, 97030.

# NOTES

## Chapter 1

1. "Gallup: Seventy-Two Percent of Teens Say Abortion Wrong," November 24, 2003, WorldNetDaily.com.

2. "New National Abortion Poll Shows Majority of Americans Are Pro-Life," (December 2003 Zogby International Poll, posted January 16, 2004, 209.157.64.200/focus/f-news/1062123/posts).

3. January 23, 1994, "Young People Swell Crowd at Washington March for Life," 209.157.64.200/focus/f-religion/1064531/posts.

4. See www.standupgirl.com.

5. "Abortion: Facts at a Glance" (New York: Planned Parenthood of America), 1.

6. The Alan Guttmacher Institute website, www.agi-usa.org/pubs/fb_induced_abortion.html; *Facts in Brief*, rev. February 2000.

7. Alan Guttmacher Institute, "Induced Abortion," *Facts in Brief*, February 2002.

8. James Patterson and Peter Kim, *The Day America Told the Truth* (New York: Prentice Hall Press, 1991), 32.

9. Lydia Saad, "Americans Divided Over Abortion Debate," 18 May 1999, Gallup News Service Poll Releases; www.gallup.com/content/login.aspx?ci=3847.

10. *Family Planning Perspectives,* July–August 1996, 12.

11. Randy Alcorn, *ProLife Answers to ProChoice Arguments* (Sisters, OR: Multnomah Publishers, 2000), 313–22; "Biblical Perspectives on Unborn Children," www.epm.org/articles/aborbibl.html.

*Chapter 2*

1. "Gallup Finds Two-Thirds of Americans Believe Abortion Is Morally Wrong," June 2003, www.lifesite.net/ldn/2003/jun/03060308.html.

2. Paul Swope, "Abortion: A Failure to Communicate," *First Things,* April 1998, 31–35. See www.firstthings.com/ftissues/ft9804/articles/swope.html.

*Chapter 3*

1. Subcommittee on Separation of Powers to Senate Judiciary Committee S-158, Report, 97th Cong., 1st Session, 1981.

2. Ibid.

3. Ibid.

4. *Lovejoy Surgicenter v. Advocates for Life Ministries,* et al., 1989, testimony of Aileen Klass.

5. Alexander Tsiaras, *From Conception to Birth: A Life Unfolds* (New York: Doubleday, 2002).

6. *Missouri Revised Statutes,* chapter 1, "Laws in Force and Construction of Statutes," Section 1.205, August 28, 2003. See www.moga.state.mo.us/statutes/C000-099/0010000205.htm.

7. R. Houwink, *Data: Mirrors of Science* (New York: American Elsevier Publishing Co., Inc., 1970), 104–190.

8. Lennart Nilsson, "Drama of Life Before Birth," *Life*, 30 April 1965.

9. "The Facts of Life" (Norcross, GA: Human Development Resource Council), 2.

10. Vincent J. Collins, "Fetal Pain and Abortion: The Medical Evidence," *Studies in Law and Medicine* (Chicago: Americans United for Life, 1984), 6–7.

11. See *Newsweek*, June 9, 2003, "The War Over Fetal Rights," 40–47.

12. These are well-established scientific facts. See, for instance, Landrum Shettles and David Rorvik, *Rites of Life* (Grand Rapids: Zondervan, 1983), 41–66.

13. Scott Klusendorf, *Pro-Life 101: A Step-by-Step Guide to Making Your Case Persuasively* (Signal Hill, CA: Stand to Reason Press, 2002).

14. Justin Taylor, "Sticker Shock," *World*, January 17, 2004, 43.

### Chapter 4

1. Leonide M. Tanner, ed., "Developing Professional Parameters: Nursing and Social Work Roles in the Care of the Induced Abortion Patient," *Clinical Obstetrics and Gynecology* 14 (December 1971): 1271.

2. Paul Marx, *The Death Peddlers: War on the Unborn* (Collegeville, MN: St. John's University Press, 1971), 21.

3. *Feminists for Life Debate Handbook* (Kansas City, MO: Feminists for Life of America, n.d.), 3.

4. Carl Sagan and Ann Druyan, "Is It Possible to Be Pro-Life and Pro-Choice?" *Parade*, 22 April 1990, 4.

5. *The First Nine Months* (Colorado Springs: Focus on the Family), 3.

6. *Preview of a Birth* (Norcross, GA: Human Development Resource Center, 1991), 4.

7. See Scott Klusendorf, "Harvesting the Unborn: The Ethics of Embryo Stem Cell Research," www.str.org/free/bioethics/harvest.pdf.

8. "Deadline Extended for Comment to NIH on Stem Cells Harvesting," *Prolife Infonet*, 31 January 2000.

9. Thomas W. Hilgers, Dennis J. Horan and David Mall, eds., *New Perspectives on Human Abortion* (Frederick, MD: University Publications of America Inc./Aletheia Books, 1981), 351.

10. *Slate: Medical Examiner*, "Did I Violate the Partial-Birth Abortion Ban? A Doctor Ponders a New Era of Prosecution," by Dr. Warren M. Hern, October 22, 2003; http://slate.msn.com/id/2090215.

*Chapter 5*

1. Mortimer J. Adler, *Haves Without Have-Nots: Essays for the 21st Century on Democracy and Socialism* (New York: MacMillan, 1991), 210.
2. "Brain-Dead Woman Gives Birth," *The Oregonian*, 31 July 1987.
3. See www.michaelclancy.com/story.html.
4. Chuck Colson, "Life-and-Death Decisions: Praying for the Supremes," BreakPoint Commentary #000425, 25 April 2000.
5. HR 1997 was passed by a Senate roll call vote of 61-38, March 25, 2004.

*Chapter 6*

1. Madeline Nash, "Inside the Womb," *Time*, November 11, 2002, 68–77; Debra Rosenberg, "The War Over Fetal Rights," *Newsweek*, June 9, 2003, 40–51.
2. Mark O'Keefe, "Activists Tout Ultrasound Images to Discourage Abortion," Newhouse News Service, www.newhouse.com/archive/okeefe021903.html, © 2003.
3. Jennifer Kabbany, "Abortion vs. Ultrasound," *Washington Times,* October 29, 2003.
4. Audrey Stout, Marietta, GA, e-mail to Randy Alcorn, February 12, 2000.
5. See www.logiqlibrary.com/browseAction.cfm?productID=20; www.geddeskeepsake.com/showcase.html; www.clearviewultrasound.com/gallery.asp;firstsightultrasound.com/4d_liveSA.htm; www.gemedicalsystems.com/rad/us/4d/virtual.html; to find other images, enter the words *ultrasound, images,* and *unborn* into a search engine.
6. *Life*, August 1990.
7. Lennart Nilsson, *A Child Is Born* (New York: Delacorte Press, 1977).
8. See www.abortiontv.com/AbortionPictures1.htm.

9. Warren Hern, "Operative Procedures and Technique," *Abortion Practice* (Boulder, CO: Alpenglo Graphics, Inc., 1990), 154.

10. Naomi Wolf, "Our Bodies, Our Souls," *The New Republic,* October 16, 1995; www.epm.org/articles/naomiwolf.html.

11. *Care Net Report,* vol. 4, no. 5, November 2003, Sterling, VA.

12. Oregon Public Broadcasting, "To the Contrary," former Clinton administration staffer Maria Echaveste, et al., January 4, 2004.

*Chapter 7*

1. Mary Fischer, "A New Look at Life," *Reader's Digest*, October 2003, 95–103.

2. Peter Singer, *Practical Ethics* (1979), cited in "Peter Singer in His Own Words," Accuracy in Acadamia, www.academia.org/singerquotes.html.

3. Jim Newhall, cited by Maureen O'Hagan, "Cross Hairs to Bear," *Willamette Week*, 3 May 1995.

4. Associated Press, cited in Christian Action Council's *Action Line*, March–April 1991.

5. Sharon Begley, "Do You Hear What I Hear?" *Newsweek*, Special Summer Edition 1991, 12.

6. Ibid.

7. T. Verney and J. Kelley, *The Secret Life of the Unborn Child* (New York: Delta Books, 1981).

8. H. B. Valman and J. F. Pearson, "What the Fetus Feels." (This is a printed article with no reference to the publication it appeared in. Dr. Valman is consultant pediatrician at Northwick Park Hospital and Clinical Research Center in Harrow; Pearson is senior lecturer and consultant obstetrician and gynecologist at Welsh National School of Medicine in Cardiff.)

9. John Willke, *Abortion Questions and Answers* (Cincinnati, OH: Hayes Publishing Co., 1988), 53.

10. Begley, "Do You Hear?" 14.

11. Peter Singer, "Sanctity of Life or Quality of Life," *Pediatrics*, July 1983, 129.

12. Singer, "Taking Life: Humans," http://www.petersingerlinks.com/taking.htm; excerpted from Singer, *Practical Ethics* (New York: Cambridge University Press, 1993).

13. Charles Hartshorne, "Concerning Abortion: An Attempt at a Rational View," *The Christian Century*, 21 January 1981, 42–45.

14. David Boonin, *A Defense of Abortion* (New York: Cambridge University Press, 2003), 5–9.

15. *Feminists for Life Debate Handbook* (Kansas City, MO: Feminists for Life of America, n.d.), 9.

16. Quoted by George Will, *The Pursuit of Happiness and Other Sobering Thoughts* (New York: Harper Colophon, 1978), 62–63.

### Chapter 8

1. Kate Michelman, quoted in *The New York Times*, May 10, 1988.

2. *Feminists for Life Debate Handbook* (Kansas City, MO: Feminists for Life of America, n.d.), 17.

3. Rosemary Bottcher, "Feminism: Bewitched by Abortion," in *To Rescue the Future*, ed. Dave Andrusko (New York: Life Cycle Books, 1983).

4. See www.feministsforlife.org/news/commonw.htm.

5. Susan B. Anthony, *The Revolution*, July 8, 1869, 4.

6. Mattie Brinkerhoff, *The Revolution*, April 9, 1868, 215–16.

7. Elasah Drogin, *Margaret Sanger: Father of Modern Society*, (CUL Publications, 1989), 11–13.

8. R. C. Sproul, *Abortion: A Rational Look at an Emotional Issue* (Colorado Springs, CO: NavPress, 1990), 117–18.

9. Guy M. Condon, "You Say Choice, I Say Murder," *Christianity Today*, June 24, 1991, 22.

10. Mary Ann Schaefer, quoted by Catherine and William Odell, *The First Human Right* (Toronto: Life Cycle Books, 1983), 39–40.

11. *The American Feminist*, Spring 2003, 14, 17.
12. "Abortion and Moral Beliefs: A Survey of American Opinion," conducted by the Gallup Organization, 1991, 4–7.
13. Willke, "Woman's Movement," 3.
14. Condon, "You Say Choice," 23.
15. Robert Stone, "Women Endangered Species in India," *The Oregonian,* March 14, 1989, B7.
16. Jo McGowan, "In India They Abort Females," *Newsweek*, February 13, 1989.
17. *Straits Times* report, Beijing, February 7, 2000; related stories at www.lifesite.net.
18. *Medical World News*, December 1, 1975, 45. See also *Newsweek,* "Brave New Babies," February 1, 2004.

### Chapter 9

1. Mary O'Brien Drum, "Meeting in the Radical Middle," *Sojourners,* November 1980, 23.
2. Nat Brandt, *The Town That Started the Civil War* (New York: Syracuse University Press, 1990); Thomas Clarkson, *Slavery and Commerce of the Human Species* (Miami, FL: Mnemosyne Publ. Co., 1969); Austin Willey, *The History of the Anti-Slavery Cause* (Portland, ME: Brown Thurston Publ., reprinted by Mnemosyne Publ. Co., Miami, FL, 1886).

### Chapter 10

1. See Robert Jay Lifton, *The Nazi Doctors: Medical Killing and the Psychology of Genocide* (New York: Basic Books, 1986).
2. See www.teen-aid.org/Links.htm; www.abstinencedu.com; www.abednet.org; www.PureRevolution.com.

### Chapter 11

1. Serrin M. Foster, "Women Deserve Better Than Abortion," *Respect Life,* 2003.
2. Quoted by Mary Meehan, "The Ex-Abortionists: Why They Quit," *Human Life Review* (Spring–Summer 2000), 12.

3. Elizabeth Shadigan, MD, testimony before the Senate sub-committee on science, technology, and space's hearing to investigate the physical and psychological effects of abortion on women; cited in "Witnesses Ask U.S. Senate for Research into Side Effects of Abortion on Women," *Culture & Cosmos*, vol. 1, no. 30, March 9, 2004.

4. Brent Rooney and Byron C. Calhoun, MD, "Induced Abortion and Risk of Later Premature Births," *Journal of American Physicians and Surgeons*, vol. 8, no. 2, Summer 2003.

5. S. Linn, "The Relationship Between Induced Abortion and Outcome of Subsequent Pregnancies," *American Journal of Obstetrics and Gynecology*, May 15, 1983, 136–40.

6. John A. Richardson and Geoffrey Dixon, "Effects of Legal Termination on Subsequent Pregnancy," *British Medical Journal* (1976): 1303–4.

7. B. Luke, *Every Pregnant Woman's Guide to Preventing Premature Birth* (New York: Times Books, 1995); E. Ring-Cassidy, *Woman's Health After Abortion* (Toronto: de Veber Institute, 2002).

8. *Family Planning Perspectives*, March–April 1983, 85–86.

9. U.S. Department of Health and Human Services, *Morbidity and Mortality Weekly Report* 42 (SS-6) 73–85 (December 17, 1993; April 1984).

10. Ann Aschengrau Levin, "Ectopic Pregnancy and Prior Induced Abortion," *American Journal of Public Health* (March 1982): 253.

11. "Ectopic Pregnancy: Prognosis for Subsequent Fertility," www.physicianeducation.org. Accessed March 1, 2004.

12. Centers for Disease Control, Press Release, May 1, 2001, "CDC Reports Highlights Selected Racial and Ethnic Pregnancy-Related Death Rates," http://www.cdc.gov/od/oc/media/pressrel/r010511.htm.

13. Allan Osser, MD, and Kenneth Persson, MD, "Postabortal Pelvic Infection Associated with Chlamydia Tracomatis and

the Influence of Humoral Immunity," *American Journal of Obstetrics and Gynecology* (November 1984): 669–703.

14. Lars Heisterberg, MD, et al., "Sequelae of Induced First-Trimester Abortion," *American Journal of Obstetrics and Gynecology* (July 1986): 79.

15. Anath, CV, et al.: "The Association of Placenta Previa with History of Cesarean Delivery and Abortion: A Meta-Analysis," *American Journal of Obstetrics and Gynecology* (November 1997): 1071–78.

16. Jeffrey M. Barrett, MD, "Induced Abortion: A Risk Factor for Placental Previa," *American Journal of Obstetrics and Gynecology* (December 1981): 769.

17. David Reardon, *Aborted Women: Silent No More* (Westchester, IL: Crossway Books, 1987), 106.

18. F. Parazzini, et al., "Reproductive Factors and the Risk of Invasive and Intraepithelial Cervical Neoplasia," *British Journal of Cancer*, 59:805–9 (1989); H. L. Stewart, et al., "Epidemiology of Cancers of the Uterine Cervix and Corpus, Breast and Ovary in Israel and New York City," *Journal of the National Cancer Institute* 37(i):1–96; I. Fujimoto et al., "Epidemiologic Study of Carcinoma in Situ of the Cervix," *Journal of Reproductive Medicine* 30(7):535 (July 1985); C. LaVecchia, et al., "Reproductive Factors and the Risk of Hepatocellular Carcinoma in Women," *International Journal of Cancer*, 52:351, 1992.

19. Dr. Joel Brind, "Comprehensive Review and Meta-Analysis of the Abortion/Breast Cancer Link"; http://members.aol.com/DFjoseph/brind.html.

20. Brinton LA, Hoover R, Fraumeni IF, Ir. (1983) *British Journal of Cancer*, 47:757–62.

21. Linn, "Outcome of Subsequent Pregnancies," 136–40.

22. John A. Richardson and Geoffrey Dixon, "Effects of Legal Termination on Subsequent Pregnancy," *British Medical Journal* (1976): 1303–4.

23. Herman, *Trauma and Recovery*, (New York: Basic Books, 1992), 34; "Abortion's Adverse Physical and Psychological Effects on Women" (list of studies).

24. For this and other studies see Elliot Institute, www.afterabortion.org.

25. David C. Reardon, "Major Psychological Sequelae of Abortion," 1997, Elliot Institute.

26. "Tearing Down the Wall," *LifeSupport*, Spring–Summer 1991, 1–3.

27. See Alcorn, *ProLife Answers*, 118–20, 285–86.

28. Free information and counseling is available via www.lifeissues.org/men/.

29. Gissler M, Berg C, Bouvier-Colle MH, Buekens P., "Pregnancy-Associated Mortality After Birth, Spontaneous Abortion or Induced Abortion in Finland, 1987–2000," Am J Ob-Gyn 2004; 190:422–27.

30. Centers for Disease Control, *Morbidity and Mortality Weekly Report*, 52 (SS12); 1–32, "Abortion Surveillance—United States, 2000," 32.

31. James A. Miller, "A Tale of Two Abortions," *Human Life International Reports*, March 1991, 1.

32. John Willke, *Abortion Questions and Answers* (Cincinnati, OH: Hayes Publishing Co., 1988), 99; Brian Clowes, *Facts of Life*, "Maternal Deaths Due to Abortion," Human Life International; 2nd ed. (June 2001).

33. Wanda Franz, "Abortion Associated with Heightened Mortality Rate, Study Reveals," www.nrlc.org/news/2002/NRL09/franz.html.

34. Elizabeth Ring-Cassidy and Ian Gentles, *Women's Health After Abortion: The Medical and Psychological Evidence*, 2nd ed. (de Veber Institute, 2003), www.deveber.org.

35. "Key Facts About Abortion," Elliot Institute, n.d., www.afterabortion.org.

### Chapter 12

1. Shettles and Rorvik, *Rites of Life* (Grand Rapids, MI: Zondervan, 1983), 129.

## Chapter 13

1. Jean Staker Garton, *Who Broke the Baby?* (Minneapolis, MN: Bethany House Publishers, 1979), 76.

2. "Who Has Abortions?" The Alan Guttmacher Institute, www.agi-usa.org/pubs/fb_induced_abortion.html.

3. "Abortion: Facts at a Glance," Planned Parenthood Federation of America, n.d., 1.

4. John Willke, *Abortion Questions and Answers* (Cincinnati, OH: Hayes Publishing Co., 1988), 146–50.

5. Sue Reily, "Life Uneasy for Woman at Center of Abortion Ruling," *The Oregonian*, 9 May 1989, A2.

6. "Jane Roe Wants to Make Legal History Again," June 21 2003, www.theage.com.au/articles/2003/06/20/1055828492398.html .

7. *Feminists for Life Debate Handbook* (Kansas City, MO: Feminists for Life of America, n.d.), 14.

8. Frederica Mathewes-Green, "Ask the Victims," *Citizen Magazine 2000*, family.org/cforum/citizenmag/features/a0013078.cfm.

## Chapter 14

1. W. Peacock, "Active Voluntary Euthanasia," *Issues in Law and Medicine*, 1987. Cited by John Willke, *Abortion Questions and Answers* (Cincinnati, OH: Hayes Publishing Co., 1988), 212.

2. National Vital Statistics Report, vol. 48, no. 3, March 28, 2000.

3. March of Dimes Foundation, 2003, www.marchofdimes.com/professionals/681_1164.asp.

4. World Congress of Families Update, vol. 3, issue 1119, March 2002, www.worldcongress.org/WCFUpdate/Archive03/wcf_update_311.htm citing R. E. Gilbert, et al., "Screening for Down's Syndrome: Effects, Safety, and Cost-Effectiveness of First- and Second-Trimester Strategies"; and Euan M. Wallace and Sheila Mulvey, "Commentary: Results May Not Be Widely Applicable," BMJ 2001; 323:1–6 (25 August 2001); www.bmj.com.

5. Willke, *Abortion Questions*, 211.

6. "Born Unwanted: Developmental Consequences for Children of Unwanted Pregnancies," Planned Parenthood Federation of America, n.d.

7. The Michael Fund, 400 Penn Center, Pittsburgh, PA 15146.

## Chapter 15

1. Report of the National Center of Child Abuse and Neglect, U.S. Department of Health and Human Services, 1973–1982.

2. See www.acf.hhs.gov/programs/cb/publications/cm01/chapterthree.htm#victim.

3. Edward Lenoski, *Heartbeat* 3 (December 1980); cited by John Willke, *Abortion Questions and Answers* (Cincinnati, OH: Hayes Publishing Co., 1988), 140–41.

4. Nancy Michels, *Helping Women Recover from Abortion* (Minneapolis, MN: Bethany House Publishers, 1988), 168.

5. Philip G. Ney, "A Consideration of Abortion Survivors," *Child Psychiatry and Human Development* (Spring 1983): 172–73.

6. Philip G. Ney, "Relationship Between Abortion and Child Abuse," *Canadian Journal of Psychiatry* (November 1979): 611–12.

7. Michels, *Helping Women Recover,* 169–70.

8. Cited by James Dobson, *Focus on the Family* radio broadcast, 21 June 1991.

9. Peter Singer, *Rethinking Life and Death* (New York: St. Martin's Griffin, 1996), 217.

## Chapter 17

1. Frederica Mathewes-Green, *Real Choices* (Sisters, OR: Multnomah Publishers, 1995), 19.

2. David Reardon, *Aborted Women: Silent No More* (Westchester, IL: Crossway Books, 1987), 10.

3. *1989 Adoption Factbook,* The National Council for Adoption (Washington, DC, June 1989), 158. These figures are relatively the same in 2000, per phone conversation on 5/8/00 with a representative of NCFA, confirming at least one million couples

of childbearing age constitute the minimum adoption
demand for newborns in the U.S.

4. Cited by Charmaine Yoest, "Why Is Adoption So Difficult?"
   *Focus on the Family Citizen*, 17 December 1990, 10.
5. Testimonies of clinic workers in *The Abortion Providers*, a
   video produced by Pro-Life Action League, Chicago.
   Confirmed by former abortion clinic owner Carol Everett, in
   private telephone conversation between her, Frank Peretti,
   and the author on May 24, 1991.
6. Mathewes-Green, *Real Choices*, 14–15.
7. Yoest, "Why Is Adoption So Difficult?" 10.
8. See www.bethany.org; www.cwa.org/links.html;
   www.preciouskids.org/adopt/resources.html;
   www.adopting.com/info.html.
9. See http://encyclopedia.adoption.com.
10. Swopes, "Aborton: A Failure to Communicate,"
    www.firstthings.com/ftissues/ft9804/articles/swope.html.

## Chapter 18

1. *Family Planning Perspectives*, July–August 1996, 12.
2. See www.lifeservices.org/pace.htm;
   www.afterabortion.org/healing; call 1-888-486-HOPE for free
   confidential advice; resource list for postabortion needs:
   www.afterabortion.org/resourc.html.

## Chapter 20

1. Care Net's option line is 1-800-395-HELP (4351); on-line
   help at www.optionline.org.
2. See www.catholic.net/RCC/Prolife/prolife1.html.
3. Eternal Perspective Ministries, www.epm.org, info@epm.org,
   (503) 663-6481; 2229 E. Burnside #23, Gresham, OR 97030.
4. For information on the National Memorial for the Unborn,
   see www.atcmag.com/v1n4/article6.asp; church rose garden at
   www.epm.org/articles/rosegard.html.

5. My book *ProLife Answers to ProChoice Arguments* is a thorough response to pro-choice claims, backed up with eight hundred citations.

6. See Alcorn, *ProLife Answers*, Appendix K: ProLife Resources, 381–404; see www.epm.org/proliferesources.html. An extremely helpful information source is the Ultimate Pro-Life Resource List at www.prolife.org/ultimate. To subscribe to regular prolife information emails, send the message "subscribe" to infonet-list-request@lists.prolife.org.

7. Randy Alcorn, *Does the Birth Control Pill Cause Abortions?* (Gresham, OR: Eternal Perspective Ministries, 1997, 2000, 2004), www.epm.org/bcp.html; Drs. Walter Larimore and Joseph Stanford, "Postfertilization Effects of Oral Contraceptives and Their Relation to Informed Consent," *Archives of Family Medicine* 2000; 9:133; Dr. Walter L. Larimore, "The Growing Debate About the Abortifacient Effect of the Birth Control Pill and the Principle of Double Effect," *Ethics and Medicine Journal*, January 2000; 16(1):23–30. Also available in updated format at www.epm.org/articles/pilldebate.html.

8. See www.family.org/pregnancy/general/A0028208.html.

9. Many pro-life resources are available on-line, including our organization's at www.epm.org/prolife.html. All articles I've written and everything at our website are freely available for church and ministry use, including a small-group Bible study lesson at www.epm.org/articles/aboleson.html, and a complete sample of a creative pro-life church service and message at www.epm.org/articles/abosergs.html.

10. *Life Is Sacred* and other pro-life resources, www.family.org/resources/itempg.cfm?itemid=1072.

11. See www.abortionno.org/pdf/order.pdf.

## "This book is must reading for every citizen in our nation—prolife or prochoice."

—CAROL EVERETT, former abortion clinic owner and author of *Blood Money: Getting Rich Off a Woman's Right to Choose*

ISBN 1-57673-751-9

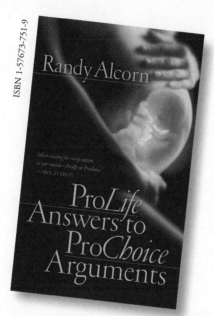

As politicians, citizens, and families continue the raging national debate about whether it's proper to end human life in the womb, resources like Randy Alcorn's *ProLife Answers to ProChoice Arguments* have proven invaluable. This revised and updated guide offers timely information and inspiration from a "sanctity of life" perspective. Real answers to real questions appear in a logical and concise form. The final chapter—"Fifty Ways to Help Unborn Babies and Their Mothers"—is worth the price of the book alone.

# Big Change titles from...
## RANDY ALCORN

### The Treasure Principle
Discovering the Secret of Joyful Giving

Bestselling author Randy Alcorn uncovers the revolutionary key to spiritual transformation: joyful giving! Jesus' life-changing formula guarantees not only kingdom impact, but immediate pleasure and eternal rewards.
ISBN 1-57673-780-2

The Treasure Principle Bible Study
ISBN 1-59052-187-0

### The Grace and Truth Paradox
Responding with Christlike Balance

Living like Christ is a lot to ask! Discover Randy Alcorn's two-point checklist of Christlikeness—and begin to measure everything by the simple test of grace and truth.
ISBN 1-59052-065-3

### The Purity Principle
God's Safeguards for Life's Dangerous Trails

Some people have given up on purity. Some have never tried. Bestselling author Randy Alcorn shows us why, in this culture of impurity, the stakes are so high—and what we can do to experience the freedom of purity.
ISBN 1-59052-195-1

# from *Fiction* Randy Alcorn

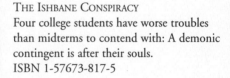

### The Ishbane Conspiracy
Four college students have worse troubles than midterms to contend with: A demonic contingent is after their souls.
ISBN 1-57673-817-5

### Lord Foulgrin's Letters
*Lord Foulgrin's Letters* invites believers to eavesdrop on their worst Enemy, learn his strategies and tricks, and discover how to ward off his devilish attacks.
ISBN 1-57673-679-2

### Deadline
After tragedy strikes those closest to him, journalist Jake Woods is drawn into a complex murder investigation that forces him to ultimately seek answers to the meaning of his existence.
ISBN 1-57673-316-5

### Dominion
When two murders drag a columnist into the world of gangs and racial conflict, he seeks revenge for the killings, and answers to the hard issues regarding race and faith.
ISBN 1-57673-661-X